TEACHING

FOR DEMOCRATIC CITIZENSHIP

KEN OSBORNE

Canadian Cataloguing in Publication Data

Osborne, Kenneth, 1936–
Teaching for democratic citizenship

(Our schools/our selves monograph series; 8)
Includes bibliographical references.
ISBN 0–921908–09–1

1. Citizenship – Study and teaching.
2. Democracy – Study and teaching. 3. Education – Aims and Objectives. 4. Teaching. I. Our Schools/Our Selves Education Foundation.
II. Title.

LC1091.072 1991 370.11'5 C91–095599–9

This book is published by Our Schools/Our Selves Education Foundation, 1698 Gerrard Street East, Toronto, Ontario, M4L 2B2.

For subscribers to Our Schools/Our Selves: a magazine for Canadian education activists, this is issue #19–20 (a double issue), the third and fourth issues of volume 3.

The subscription series Our Schools/Our Selves (ISSN 0840–7339) is published 8 times a year. Second class mail registration number 8010. Mailed at Centre Ville, Montréal, Québec.

Design and typesetting: Tobin MacIntosh.

Our Schools/Our Selves production: Heather Alden, David Clanfield, Doug Little, Tobin MacIntosh, George Martell, Harry Smaller.

Printed in Canada by La maîtresse d'école inc., Montréal, Québec.

Acknowledgments

Over the years I have known many good teachers. I have seen them in action, worked with them as a colleague, and talked about teaching with them. I began teaching in 1961 and continue to spend a good deal of time in schools. My work at the University of Manitoba gives me the opportunity to read a good deal of what has been written about teaching. As a result, I no longer know how my ideas originated. Did they come from my own experience with students? From friends and colleagues? From reading? From pure reflection? Presumably, they come from some combination of all these sources. I am sure of one thing: there is nothing in this book that cannot be done in the classroom, and, for that matter, that has not been done somewhere.

I owe a good deal to friends and colleagues with whom I have been associated over some thirty years of teaching. I owe even more to my wife, Janet, whose ability to see whether the emperor is wearing any clothes has all these years kept me from drowning in the theoretical swamps that so often seem to plague writing on education. I have also benefitted from the comments and questions of David Clandfield, Bob Davis, Doug Little, George Martell and Harry Smaller. As they will be the first to realize, I have not always accepted their suggestions, but they forced me to think. Writing this book has been a very useful exercise for me. Whether it has any wider use is for others to decide.

Though they are certainly not responsible for its inevitable weaknesses, I would like to dedicate this book to all my friends and colleagues in teaching, in Winnipeg and elsewhere.

Winnipeg
October 1991

K.O.

Contents

Introduction

Books about teaching are not generally seen as a good read. Why, then, write this one? Student-teachers read books on teaching because they have to — and then promptly forget them. Qualified teachers ignore them as having nothing useful to say. Most parents do not know that they exist. And we prefer to keep students totally in the dark when it comes to questions of how they should be taught. So, the question arises: Why should anyone read this book? It is not a question I can answer, but I can say why I have written it and why I think it might prove useful.

First, teaching is obviously important. How students are taught influences their attitude to education and plays an important part in determining whether they will succeed or fail in school. This does not mean that *how* we teach is more important than *what* we teach, as some enthusiasts like to insist. Still, it is obvious that how we teach does influence students' reaction to what we teach. We can all think of teachers whose style, approach and personality influenced us. My enthusiasm for history, for example, began not because of the subject but because of one particular teacher.

Second, a style of teaching acts as a form of subject-matter in its own right. As some examples in this book demonstrate, students learn more from how they are taught than they or their teachers often realize. If, for example, a subject is taught only by way of notes on the overhead projector, end-of-chapter questions from the textbook, and the occasional out of date film, it will not be surprising if students find it dull and boring. Nor will it be surprising if they associate learning in general, and schooling in particular, with pointless and tedious exercises in memorizing and copying,

Third, a good deal has been written about teaching over the years. Some of it is useful and some of it is best left on the library shelves. Much of the useful work however, is written in the pretentious and complicated language that education seems to bring out in people, and as a result has a limited audience. It deserves to be more widely known, not least by teachers. One of the many contradictions in education is that research on teaching is rarely done by teachers. It is done on them rather than by them and is almost never addressed to them. One of the purposes of this book is to make at least some of the research more accessible to teachers and student-teachers.

It is not enough to make recent research on teaching available only to teachers, however. A fourth reason for writing this book is to open the question of teaching to as wide an audience as possible. Teaching is too important to be left to teachers and researchers. It should be a major interest of students themselves, of parents, and of anyone interested in what schools do and do not do and what they contribute to the society that supports them. It should be of particular concern to all those interested in the relationship between schooling and social class, gender and race. How we teach does much to decide who succeeds and who fails in schools. And the better that children do in school, even as early as in kindergarten, the more interesting and stimulating the teaching they receive is likely to be. There is a close connection between being a 'good' student (or a 'bad' one) and receiving good (or bad) teaching.

These, then, are four of the reasons that led me to write this book, though they are not the most important. My fundamental reason for writing it, and the one that shapes this book from beginning to end, flows from the conviction that how we teach students (as well as what we teach them) has a lot to do with the kinds of citizens they become. Teaching is an important shaper of citizenship. If we want to see the emergence of a truly democratic society, one that goes beyond the liberal democracy that now exists, then we must pay attention to teaching. The title of this book is important. Teaching is not just about helping students pass their exams, complete high school, get a good job, or become a better person. Important as they are, these are all individual goals. While not ignoring them, we must never forget that teaching also has a social purpose. Teaching must be guided by a vision of citizenship.

Citizenship is not, it must be said, a word that generates excitement. Most people seem to put it in the same category as clean underwear: a useful and even desirable thing to have, but dull and respectable and not worth talking about. In school, it is usually accompanied by the word "responsible." After all no-one can object to responsible citizenship as a goal of education, if only because no-one knows what it really means. Most often, in the school context, responsible citizens are those who do their homework, obey their teachers, run for student council, help maintain school spirit and pick up an award or two. Above all, they do not rock the boat. The same is generally true in the world outside the school, where responsible citizens are those who do what they are told and do not ask too many awkward questions. In the words of a Canadian history text, citizens are supposed to be "hard-working, temperate and peaceable" (Osborne, 1981). Most of us suspect that there is more to citizenship than this. Indeed, our failure to get beyond this may be largely responsible for the present high level of frustration with the way parliamentary democracy is working.

Traditionally, Canadian schools have seen citizenship in passive terms. They have emphasized obedience and conformity for most students, with only a select, allegedly academic few being encouraged to think for themselves. By and large, classrooms mostly are friendlier places than they were in the past, but their power relationships have not changed. Their fundamental message is still: sit down, shut up, this is important, it will be on the test. Indeed, historians of education have shown us that one of the driving forces behind compulsory schooling was the concern of the powerful for social control. The British used to call it "gentling the masses." In Canada it was called responsible citizenship. Attendance at school was intended to promote in children the belief that all was for the best in the best of all possible worlds, and to show them how to keep it so. Schools would civilise the potential trouble-makers and rebels and help the rich and powerful sleep soundly in their beds.

All the same, the supporters of compulsory schooling did at least have a view of citizenship, no matter how conservative. And there have always been those who saw the potential of education for social change. Schools were never as conservative as they were supposed to be. When working people supported the call for compulsory schooling, it was not because they were the dupes of those higher up the social ladder. Marx and Engels, we should remember, even made compulsory education one of the planks of the *Communist Manifesto*.

But today, citizenship has fallen out of favour. Now we are told that education must promote productivity and the entrepreneurial spirit, and, to use the new magic word, "competitiveness". Education is now seen as the foundation for success in the dog-eat-dog world of the international economy. How will we cope with free trade? With the Japanese and the Europeans? How do we ensure that our prime ministers can continue to bask in their membership of the exclusive G7? By being competitive. And we do that by reforming our education system.

The enthusiasts for competitiveness see education as the process of shaping workers and producers, and to some extent consumers. In their view education must serve the "needs of the economy" — and not just the economy in the abstract, but a specific economy in a specific place at a specific point in time and from a specific perspective. The "needs of the economy" really means the needs of the corporate elite and their political and media allies, who now largely define our political and economic agenda. In this kind of education, the key words are accountability, effectiveness, standards, quality, literacy, testing. These are all unobjectionable when taken out of context. Who could object to education being effective and of high quality? In their actual content, however, they point in a clear direction. How will quality be defined, effectiveness measured and accountability achieved? By whom?

The answers most often heard in our political and media arenas say nothing about citizenship. To the efficiency experts of the new right such a notion gets in the way of productive economic priorities. It seems at best woolly and sentimental; at worst, vapid and empty of meaning. To the social reformers of the left, it carries with it a historical baggage of conformist civics and conservative conditioning. To teachers themselves it seems irrelevant to their tasks of coping with the daily grind of the classroom.

In response, I want to argue that we must return to the original language of citizenship. We must strip the word of its conservative associations and restore its radical meaning. In the era of the American and French Revolutions, citizenship was a revolutionary word. It was no coincidence that the French Revolutionaries chose "citizen" as a form of address. It showed that people were no longer subjects placed under the monarch, but were citizens, with fundamental rights to freedom and equality, and above all to an active and shared involvement in the running of their community.

This view of citizenship emerged from struggle. The right to vote, to organize, to enjoy equal status before the law, to enjoy social rights such as health care, were never simply handed over by the powerful. They were won through struggle. They have to be preserved, protected and, indeed, extended. We are still far from overcoming the inequalities of race, class and gender, for example. Even some of the rights that we have won are under attack.

At the same time, citizenship is not simply a matter of rights. It brings with it obligations and responsibilities, and the biggest responsibility is that of active, critical participation at all levels of society. As things stand, we are far from achieving the reality of democracy. Our political institutions are dominated by middle-class men.With a few exceptions, women, minorities, working people and native people are left outside the power structure. Our economic institutions do not even have the appearance of democratic control. The workplace, for example, is where most Canadians spend much of their lives (when not unemployed), but it is also one of the most undemocratic places in Canada. In social terms we still live with serious inequalities of wealth, power, influence and the full enjoyment of human potential. It is not surprising that so many Canadians feel that there is something wrong with Canadian political life.

If democratic citizenship is to become a reality, many things must change, including the schools. Citizenship is not only a status that one acquires at birth, to be recorded on a passport or in the census. It is also learned. It depends on the possession of knowledge, values and abilities that have to be taught. So far, we have taught a restricted, *status quo* version of citizenship. We have not, for the most part, taught the kind of citizenship that stresses the importance of active, critical participation directed towards the enhancement of democratic values.

The argument of this book is based upon a conviction that democracy is not defined simply by the existence of certain institutions, such as free elections and the rule of law. These are obviously of fundamental importance, but they do not define democracy so much as make it possible. Democracy must be extended beyond the political into the social and economic realm. As the Canadian political theorist C.B. Macpherson put it, democracy demands "a change in people's consciousness (or unconsciousness) from seeing themselves and acting as essentially consumers, to seeing themselves and acting as exerters and enjoyers of the exertion and development of their capacities." (Macpherson, 1976:99)

If people are to see themselves not as consumers but rather as exerters and enjoyers, the process must begin early. The school system is one of the places where it can begin. Schools must be dedicated to the promotion of a citizenship that is committed to the values of community, cooperation, participation and democracy. This cannot be left only to the teachers and to the education experts — especially not to the experts. It concerns us all, including those who know only too well that they and their children have not been well served by the schools. It is a question that becomes even more urgent when a particular economic and political agenda is being imposed on schools.

All of which is an attempt to explain why I have written this book. Although the book deals with teaching, its driving force is its concern for democratic citizenship. The argument can be stated as a series of propositions.

1. Schools play an important part in the establishment, maintenance and possible transformation of citizenship ideals and practices.

2. Schools propogate citizenship through what they teach (the curriculum), through how they teach (pedagogy), and through the interaction between the what and the how (often called the "hidden curriculum" of rules, regulations, expectations, and so forth).

3. Pedagogy, — the way subject-matter is selected, organized and presented to students — delivers powerful messages about the kind of citizenship that is valued inside and outside the school.

4. Citizenship as it currently exists in Canada falls short of the democratic ideal.

5. Schools can do something — not everything but certainly more than they now do — to improve the quality of citizenship.

In pursuing this argument, I have chosen to concentrate on the question of teaching. I have said little about democratic citizenship as such. This is a subject that deserves a book to itself, and has in fact had many devoted to it. Derek Heater has given us one of the most recent and most useful (Heater, 1990). What I mean by democratic citizenship should be clear in the chapters that follow. My main concern, however, has been with teaching and I have tried to show what teaching can be.

Most books about teaching do not seem to have been very helpful to those they should have helped. Some are written by psychologists who seem to wish to reduce students, whom they call learners, to the status of laboratory rats and pigeons. Some are written by theorists who become so fascinated with theory that they lose all sight of the classroom. Some consist of prescriptions and recipes that rarely go beyond the obvious. And obviously I'm hoping to avoid all these pitfalls. The most interesting and popular books about teaching usually describe a charismatic teacher struggling successfully against overwhelming odds. These latter books are readable, and even uplifting, but it is difficult to apply them to other contexts. What I have tried to do in this book is to present an approach to teaching that can be realized across a whole educational system.

Ever since I began working as a teacher over thirty years ago, I have been preoccupied with a question once asked by H.G. Wells: "What on earth am I up to here? Why am I giving these particular lessons in this particular way? If human society is anything more than a fit of collective insanity in the animal kingdom, what is teaching for?" This book is part of a continuing attempt to answer Wells' question. Whether I have been successful, others must judge.

Chapter One

THE IMPORTANCE OF PEDAGOGY

Teaching is important. The theory and practice of teaching form a vital part of any theory of education, and a worthwhile theory of education must in turn form part of a wider theory of society: what it is, what it might be and how we get there. Anyone who believes that there is a connection between education and citizenship, cannot afford to ignore the influence of teaching.

In practice, however, we have paid much more attention to what the schools are supposed to teach, than to how they might teach it. The content of the curriculum has held the spotlight. How students will learn it, and how teachers should teach it, might attract a few pages in a curriculum guide or a technical manual, but little else.

We are coming to realize what common-sense and personal experience have told us all along: what we learn is influenced by how we learn it. It is not that the *how* is more important than the *what*, or *vice versa*, but rather that the two are inseparably connected. Educational liberals sometimes claim that how we teach is the supremely important question, that *process* is more important than *product*. It is a silly argument. Obviously, *product* is important: what students learn does matter; some subjects are more valuable than others. In *Educating Citizens* I tried to describe what the content of education should be. My point here is to argue that *how* this content is taught and learned is also important — not necessarily more important, but important nonetheless. At the very least, teaching influences what and how students learn. More fundamentally, it also delivers a set of messages about power, authority, work and learning. It can, in fact, itself become the curriculum so far as student learning is concerned.

I once visited a classroom and, not knowing what subject was due to be taught, asked a boy sitting next to me what he was learning in the class. It proved to be an interesting way to frame the question. Had I asked what subject was being taught, he would have told me social studies, since that was in fact the case. But, on being asked what he was learning, he gave me an unexpected but honest answer. "To take notes off the overhead projector," he said, and that was indeed what happened for the whole period, as the students diligently copied notes from the screen. The teacher thought he was teaching social studies: at least one student knew better. The process was in fact more subtle than even the student realized, for, in copying notes, he was also learning to follow instructions, to do apparently pointless work to fulfil his work quota, and to do so without complaining. For this student, the curriculum was not the actual historical topic on which he was copying down notes, but the power-relationship, the work expectations and the definition of what it meant to learn that existed in the classroom.

This example illustrates four propositions that demonstrate the importance of teaching, or pedagogy, to use the word that will appear often in this book:

1. Students can learn from how we teach as well as from what we teach.

2. Students do learn crucial lessons from how we teach that have lasting effects.

3. Decisions on how we teach reflect basic fundamental philosophical and political choices.

4. A wider and more varied pedagogy will make classrooms more interesting, rewarding and effective.

The Elements of Pedagogy

Before pursuing these arguments, it will be helpful to say a little about what I mean by pedagogy. The dictionary defines it as the "science of teaching" and, essentially, I am using the word to mean teaching. This itself, however, needs further explanation, since the word "teaching" hides as much as it reveals. The standard image of teaching is still that of someone standing at the front of a room, chalk in hand (or these days, overhead projector at the ready), talking to, or at, an audience of some thirty or so younger people. There is, of course, far more to teaching than this, and one of the purposes of this book is to displace this image of teaching.

In fact, teaching consists of at least four elements. The first involves the selection of the content to be taught, for one can never totally separate method from content. A teacher might, for example, decide to use a poem in order to teach students about particular poetic techniques, or to stimulate their appreciation of poetry, or to encourage them to write their own poems, but the choice of the poem to be used is not a neutral exercise. Even in jurisdictions that impose fairly tight control over curricula, teachers still have the freedom to make some degree of emphasis and selection, to spend more time on one topic than another, to use some supplementary materials rather than others, and so on. Some degree of selection of content, then, is inescapable and it is an important element of teaching.

The second element of teaching consists of all those things that together make up the hidden curriculum: the expectations and norms of the classroom; the rules and procedures; the nature and quality of interaction between teacher and students and among the students themselves; the degree of trust and cooperation; and so on. These are largely under the control of the teacher and, given their influence on what students learn, they cannot be ignored in any consideration of teaching.

The third and fourth elements are best considered together, since they deal with the act of teaching or instruction, as generally understood. They concern such decisions as whether to lecture or to teach through discussion, whether to use groupwork, whether to use films or visiting speakers and if so which ones, whether to give students more control over their own learning, how to evaluate their work, and a host of similar instructional decisions.

There are two elements involved here: one concerns the specific teaching technique to be used (e.g., lecture, group-work, or whatever); the other concerns the overall philosophy or goal governing the selection of the particular technique. Writing specifically about social studies Massialas and Cox differentiated between "technique" and "method", and it is a distinction that can be usefully applied to all subjects. (Massialas & Cox, 1966:62) "Technique" they describe as the particular practice used in the classroom, while "method" is "the overarching attitude the teacher takes towards knowledge, the materials at hand, the learning situation, and the roles that [teacher and] students are to perform." The distinction is useful, although the terms can be confusing since, in everyday language, technique and method are used interchangeably. Thus, in what follows I will use the word "technique", but for "method" I will substitute "approach", since this suggests something broader and more inclusive.

Techniques are rarely good or bad in themselves. Their acceptability depends largely upon the approach that they are intended to serve. Their justification is contextual, though there are two obvious exceptions to this general proposition. One is that any technique that unjustly deprives students of their rights or that degrades them in any way is unacceptable. Theoretically, for example, one can think of torture or physical punishment or some other kind of coercion as a way of getting people to learn something. Anyone who has been through military training will be familiar with a variety of unpleasant techniques getting people to learn. Such techniques, however, are not included in the proposition that techniques are neither good nor bad in themselves. At the extreme, some are obviously bad and therefore to be rejected. Others might be acceptable as a form of training, but not as a feature of education.

The second exception is that many techniques become unacceptable if they are relied upon too exclusively or if they are never varied. For example, even a technique as dreary as dictating notes or putting them on an overhead transparency for students to copy could be justified in certain circumstances.

If, for example, one were preparing students for an examination, or if there were some information it was crucial for all students to have, or if students were pressed for time, or if textbooks were unavailable, it might be acceptable to dictate notes. However, if every lesson is based upon dictated or prepared notes that students have to copy, and if little or nothing else is being done, the technique is obviously being abused.

We may judge whether a particular technique is acceptable by the approach that determines its use, except in extreme cases. It is all too easy to be seduced by technique for its own sake, without thinking through its implications for one's overall approach to teaching and learning, or for its actual effectiveness. Schools have been especially prone to band-wagon enthusiasms in which one particular technique is blown out of proportion and then imposed on teachers (sometimes with their eager consent), only to fall short of the results it was expected to achieve.

The Politics of Pedagogy

Thus, pedagogy assumes a particular importance as a means for implementing an educational approach, or philosophy, to use a more familiar term. Pedagogy is not simply an add-on to content, something to be thought about once the important question of content has been answered. The choice of pedagogical techniques derives from a view of education and its purpose, a view that reflects an underlying social and political philosophy. As Paolo Freire and others have pointed out, pedagogy is not politically neutral. It carries its own messages. It puts teachers and students into certain roles. It embodies particular conceptions of power and authority. It conveys a definition of what it means to learn. It values some experiences while ignoring or condemning others. Pedagogy, in short, is a powerful form of political education, and thus carries within itself a particular view of citizenship.

Perhaps a concrete example can serve to illustrate this point. A few years ago, a number of Canadian school systems, following the long habit of importing into Canada American solutions to American problems, adopted a system of rules and regulations known as "assertive discipline." I first encountered it while watching a student-teacher teach a Grade 8 class. From time to time, for no reason that I could see, he wrote a student's name on the board. He did not say anything to the students while doing this, nor they to him, and there was something a little surrealistic about watching and hearing the student-teacher talk about ancient Sparta while writing apparently totally disconnected information on the board in the form of students' names. By the end of the class, some of the names had two or three check-marks beside them.

On talking to the student teacher, I discovered that I had come face to face with assertive discipline, a self-maintaining system by which disciplinary rules were established and a scale of punishments consistently enforced. A name on the board indicated a warning; a check-mark meant a period of detention; two check-marks meant two detentions and so on. Conversely there was a system of rewards for good behaviour: honour rolls, special awards and even lunch with the principal. A few days after this first encounter, I was in another school and here I saw the actual rules of assertive discipline. They proved to be more or less standard in all the schools that practised it. They were displayed very prominently in the classroom:

1. Students will follow the directions of all teachers and superiors the first time.

2. Students shall be on time for class.

3. Students shall have all equipment and supplies at all times.

4. Students will keep their hands, feet and other objects to themselves.

5. Students will practice good citizenship and courtesy to all students and to each other.

In light of the first four rules, good citizenship apparently meant sitting down, shutting up and obeying orders, though that is not the main point I wish to make here.

What was striking about assertive discipline was that few people saw it as anything more than one more method of keeping order in the classroom. It was discussed only in restricted terms: Did it work? Did parents like it? Was it worth the time and effort involved? These were the questions at the centre of discussion. Few people saw it as much more than just a simple disciplinary method.They did not consider its potential as an effective tool of political edcuation stressing the authority of teachers and the subordination of students. As the assertive discipline materials put it: "No child will stop me teaching for any reason." The language is provocative, even obsessive, as is the wording of the first rule: "students *will* follow the directions of *all* teachers and superiors the *first* time." Not "reasonable" or "justified" directions, but *all* directions. It is interesting to speculate on the impression students received by sitting in classrooms and in some cases walking along corridors where these rules were so conspicuously posted. They were being told surely that they were not to be trusted, that their teachers were all-powerful, and that a student's duty was to obey. As a contrast, imagine a classroom that enforced and displayed rules such as these (and that imposed detention if they were not obeyed!):

1. All students shall be as creative as possible.
2. All students must think for themselves.
3. All students shall work together and cooperate.
4. No boring textbooks or worksheets are allowed in this room.

To think in these terms is to reveal what the central message of assertive discipline really is and what its definition of education means. But, and this is the point of the example, it was rarely discussed in those terms. The questions that were asked of it were: Does it work? Is it practical?

The important questions were not asked by anyone. Teachers immersed in their immediate, everyday problems did not have the time to ask them. Administrators concerned with maintaining a well-ordered school had no interest in asking them. Parents ignorant of what happens in schools were ill-equipped to ask them. Students were not allowed to ask them.

Pedagogy, however, is not neutral. The choice of particular teaching techniques is not a simple matter of choosing which tool is best for the job. Depending upon the context in which it is used, upon the approach that it is helping to implement, a teaching technique will carry a particular message, usually embodying politically relevant values. What teachers do when they teach influences students. They often learn that they are ignorant and perhaps stupid; that their job is to learn what their teachers put in front of them and to realise that learning means memorizing and remembering; that authority is to be obeyed and orders followed. This can be done cruelly or humanely, teachers can be tyrants or benevolent despots, but the central message is one of dependence, obedience, conformity.

Alternatively, students can learn that they are intelligent, perhaps even more than they themselves realize; that what they know is important; that, although there is a lot they do not know, they can learn it without undue difficulty; that discussion, questioning and criticism are an important part of learning. The central message here is one of independence, originality, questioning.

Depending upon the pedagogical approach, students can learn that learning (and, indeed, life) is an individual business; that it is a matter of competing against others; that it involves trying to second-guess what those in power want ("Will this be on the test?"); that success means outsmarting others, by fair means or foul; that there are winners and losers and the important thing is to be a winner. Alternatively, students can learn that learning is best done in cooperation with others; that many heads are usually better than one; that cooperation is more effective, and certainly more rewarding, than competition; that learning means sharing ideas, working with others, offering one's own ideas for comment and criticism.

The choice of pedagogical approach and techniques also teaches powerful lessons about authority and power. It is obvious that teachers exercise both in the classrooms. They have power in that they are given the legal right to control students, to tell them what to do, whether they want to do it or not. They have authority to the extent that students see them as people who deserve to be heard and respected, because of their expertise or their character. They know more than their students (though not on all topics); they have more maturity and experience; they have greater control of the classroom agenda. Moreover, if their authority is questioned or challenged, they can within certain limits resort to power. They can punish students, they can impose sanctions, they can affect students' lives in many different ways. Indeed, their ability to use power is socially sanctioned; they are expected to maintain discipline and to control their classes, and the law gives them the right to do so.

Thus, students experience in a very direct way the use of both authority and power in the classroom. For many young students the classroom is the first place where they experience the application of power and authority in a more or less impartial, objective way, shorn of the emotional, personal bonds of the family. Sociologists such as Talcott Parsons, Robert Dreeben, Philip Jackson and others, have pointed out that one of the important roles schools play in society is precisely to accustom children to the norms of impartiality and universality, so that they learn that rules are rules, that not who you are but what you do is what matters. Parsons, for example, describes the school as a sort of half-way house that moves children from the subjective, personal emotion-laden world of the family to the impersonal, rational, objective world of society at large. George Orwell made the same point, though from a very different perspective. Reflecting back on his days as an eight-year old at an English upper-class boarding school, he wrote of his feelings when he returned to the school each term, after holidays: "Your home might be far from perfect, but at least it was a place ruled by love rather than by fear, where you did not have to be perpetually on your guard against the people surrounding you. At eight years old you were suddenly taken out of this warm nest and flung into a world of force and fraud and secrecy, like a gold-fish into a tank full of pike" (Orwell, 1947/1969:349).

The way in which students experience authority and power is not only important in itself, it also has important consequences for students' life beyond school and for society at large. It arises largely from the pedagogy that teachers adopt in the classroom.

Some commentators have suggested that this is an important aspect of working-class education, in that many working-class students find the academic curriculum irrelevant and uninteresting and thus provide a challenge that teachers cannot answer within the confines of the academic curriculum as it exists. Thus, for example, Robert Connell has argued that "the attempt to get most kids to swallow academic knowledge produces insurmountable problems of motivation and control, not only because of the abstractedness of the content, but also as a consequence of the formal authority relations of its teaching." (Connell, 1982:199) This and related arguments have led some educators on the left to turn away from the conventional academic curriculum and to call for a specifically working-class curriculum, despite the obvious risks of thus ghettoizing working-class students and thereby excluding them from powerful and worthwhile knowledge.

Pedagogy, then, has political consequences. Almond and Verba, for example, have argued that democratic citizenship in adult life is connected with the experience of democracy — or lack of it — in schools. In their words:

> ... if in most social situations the individual finds himself (*sic*) subservient to some authority figure, it is likely that he will expect such authority relationships in the political sphere. On the other hand, if outside the political sphere he has opportunities to participate in a wide range of social decisions, he will probably expect to be able to participate in political decisions as well. Furthermore, participation in non-political decision-making may give one the skills needed to engage in political participation. (Almond & Verba, 1965:271-2)

The implications of this for the classroom and for pedagogy need no comment.

How this operates at the classroom level was described by Sara Lightfoot some years ago. She set out to demonstrate that teachers' general world-views shape their social and political philosophies which, in turn, shape their conceptions of good teaching and thus what they do in the classroom, and that this in turn has a direct impact on their students. She described two teachers, one of whom could best be described as conservative and the other as liberal, and perhaps mildly radical. The first, Teacher A, felt that society was generally fair and open and that people could succeed if they wanted to and if they made the effort. She was critical of what she saw as permissiveness and lack of standards and believed that much was possible if people would apply themselves. Her watchwords were discipline, perseverance and effort. Teacher B, by contrast, was more critical of society. She saw systemic barriers that worked against particular groups of people no matter how hard they worked. She saw society as rewarding the privileged and penalizing the unprivileged. In her view, no matter how hard people worked, success was unlikely for many. What was needed was not self-discipline but social change, and people had therefore to work to change society in order to make it fairer and more democratic. The interest of Lightfoot's research lies in her demonstration that these political philosophies, for that is really what they are, shaped the teachers' approach to pedagogy and had an influence on their students. Teacher A, with her belief in discipline and work, emphasized orderliness, decorum and authority in the classroom. She controlled her students and they learned to follow her instructions. Teacher B, though also concerned with control, allowed more student-initiated activities, more spontaneity, and a looser pattern of discipline. The approach of the two teachers to the maintenance of authority and power was different and it had an impact on students. To quote Lightfoot:

> The approach and responsiveness of the children... reflected the educational goals and political philosophies that were unconsciously and explicitly expressed by their teachers. Teacher A spoke of cooperation, disciplined obedience, and uniformity as being primary goals of the educational process and her children expressed undifferentiated reasons for their status choices. Teacher B claimed that her primary goals for children included an expression of autonomy and self-knowl-

> edge; and her children's responses tended to be creative, aggressive, discriminating and critical. (Lightfoot, 1973:197-244)

In short, pedagogy matters. For those of us who believe that education can make a worthwhile contribution to democratic citizenship and to the quality of public life, pedagogy must become a matter of fundamental importance. It must help students become active, critical and participant citizens in their society. As the English headmaster, F.W. Sanderson, put it over sixty years ago: "We will first of all transform the life of the school, then the boys grown into men — and girls from their schools grown into women — whom their schools have enlisted into their service, will transform the life of the nation and of the whole world" (Wells, 1924:60).

Education and Citizenship

Sanderson was making the obvious link between citizenship and education and there is an obvious link between them. The school promoters of the late nineteenth and early twentieth centuries were quite clear that schools were needed for political as much as for educational reasons. The curriculum had to be designed, textbooks written, teachers trained and inspected, and of course children compelled to attend schools, in order to shape and protect a particular social order. When he introduced compulsory school attendance legislation in 1916, the Manitoba Minister of Education, R.S. Thornton, was absolutely clear about his reasons, and they were political not educational. They were phrased in terms not of what children needed, but of what the state needed:

> The reason why the state assumes to interfere in this matter is two-fold. First, it does so for its own protection. Boys and girls, the citizens of the future, must be qualified to discharge the duties of citizenship. Second, the state interferes in education for the benefit of the children themselves, who must be fitted to aid themselves so that they may not become a charge to the public. (Henley & Pampallis, 1982:81)

In making this statement, Thornton was giving voice to what has become the conventional wisdom of our own times and which took shape during the nineteenth century as the nation-state became the preferred form of political organization.

Despite the nationalist belief that nations existed almost of their own volition and were somehow self-justifying in their nature, it soon became apparent that nations had to be created and maintained. Histories had to be written and taught; languages had to be formalized; literature had to be established; traditions had to be invented; minorities had to be assimilated; loyalties had to be created. In all of this, education was crucial. Nationalism had to be disseminated and instilled. Since the young were obviously impressionable and since the future of the nation rested in their hands, they had to be taught. Thus, schools became one of the key elements of nationalist policy. Citizens, after all, did not appear from nowhere; they had to be created. In the words of one Italian nationalist: "We have made Italy; now we must make Italians" (Hobsbawm & Ranger, 1985:267).

In the process, curricula (especially in history, language and literature), textbooks, and teachers were crucial. In Manitoba, the Winnipeg School Board had clearly accepted all this. In 1914, it announced:

> On the school, more than upon any other agency, will depend the quality and the nature of the citizenship of the future; ...in the way in which the school avails itself of its opportunities depends the extent to which Canadian traditions will be appropriated, Canadian national sentiment imbibed, and Canadian standards of living adopted by the next generation of the new races that are making their home in our midst. (The School District of Winnipeg, 1914:41)

Not only did a nation have to be created and sustained, however, it also had to have its own state. Nation, territory and government were to be coterminous, and the state needed personnel: clerks, administrators, technicians, and so on. Such people needed training. They also needed the bond and stimulus of a common language and a common outlook. Thus, education was important not only for promoting nationalism; it was needed also to train the personnel necessary to the running of the national state.

The state additionally required loyalty and obedience from its citizens, and these qualities had to be learned and therefore taught. In the late 1880's, for example, the Winnipeg School Board followed the example of many other urban school systems and introduced compulsory military drill for boys. The Board took this step not for reasons of physical development or military preparedness but of character training: drill would be "of great benefit to the boys — training them to habits of attention and obedience to the general school commands." (School District of Winnipeg, 1888:14)

Finally, the nation-state could not take its existence for granted. Its sovereignty could be contested. Other states eyed it suspiciously. It had to provide for its own defence, both militarily, in the form of armies and navies, and economically, in the form of food and industrial production. Industrialization provided the key to power and prosperity. Britain, Germany, the United States pointed the way. And industrialization depended in large part upon education, not so much to provide skills and technical knowledge as to provide the necessary labour discipline. Punctuality, diligence, observance of clock-time, acceptance of the wage economy, obedience to superior authority, all had to be learned and, ideally, internalized to the point that they were taken for granted. At the very beginning of the Industrial Revolution, an English writer, William Temple, had articulated this argument, observing of children:

> There is considerable use in their being somehow or other constantly employed at least twelve hours a day, whether they earn their living or not; for by these means we hope that the rising generation will be so habituated to constant employment that it would at length prove agreeable and entertaining to them. (Thompson, 1967:84)

This view gained legitimacy from its similarity to a much older educational argument that learning should not be fun, anyway. In rejecting the ideas set forth by Rousseau in his

Emile, the Abbé Galiéni argued that "... Education is the same for man and beast. It can be reduced to two principles: to learn to put up with injustice, to learn to endure boredom... it is a question of learning the weariness of concentrating one's attention on the matter in hand." (Boyd, 1963:306-7)

All these differing but related requirements of the nation-state — nationalist feeling, trained personnel, citizenship, political attitudes, social values, security, economically appropriate dispositions — were to be met by the schools. Again the Winnipeg School Board caught the spirit of the times, noting that the day had passed when education could be seen purely in terms of intellect and culture. Education was now a social necessity. Here is the Winnipeg School Board in 1913:

> Until a comparatively recent period the schools were organized on purely academic lines and the avowed aim of education was culture and discipline. This aim has, however, been greatly enlarged within the past few years by including within its scope the development of a sense of social and civic duty, the stimulation of national and patriotic spirit, the promotion of public health and direct preparation for the occupations of life. (School District of Winnipeg, 1913:23)

Civic duty, patriotic spirit, public health, preparation for the occupations of life: it would be difficult to find a more concise statement of the role of the schools as shapers of citizenship in the newly-emerging nation-state.

However, it was a citizenship that was fundamentally passive. In the political sphere, it involved little more than voting. Politics was seen as an arena in which elite groups competed for public support, but in which people generally had little part to play. In the social sphere, it involved subscribing to the established order of society and not questioning its distribution of power and privilege. In the cultural sphere, it involved accepting the established values and rejecting any challenge to them. In the economic sphere it involved seeing private-enterprise capitalism as the most natural and most desirable economic system imaginable. Citizenship, in short, was defined in conservative terms and the schools were established as conservative institutions. Their role was neither to challenge nor transform the *status quo*, but to protect and preserve it.

It was, therefore, not especially surprising when an international survey of civic education some years ago concluded that "... nowhere has the system proved capable of producing the ideal goal of the well-informed citizenry, with democratic attitudes and values, supportive of government policies and interested in civic affairs" (Torney, 1975:21). It is not obvious that such a citizenry need necessarily be supportive of government policies, but apparently even such support has not been generated by the schools. The International Survey drew a sobering conclusion from its research: "... perhaps a hierarchical organization such as the school is not the right setting for inculcating democratic values" (Torney, 1975:21).

This conclusion is worth noting, for it draws our attention to the reality that the schools were never seriously intended to teach democratic values beyond the minimal requirements of voting, upholding law and order, and generally acting responsibly. In a world where even these basic democratic necessities are in short supply, they are not to be taken lightly. Voting does matter. Law and order are important, as is social responsibility. They can, however, be used to justify injustice and inequity. And they do obscure the reality that citizenship, with its rights and its obligations, is the result of struggle.

Citizenship must be defined in active not passive terms. It requires us to think not in terms of representation, of simply choosing representatives and then waiting for the next election, but of participation, of active involvement in the affairs of the society, at all levels. We are far from this in Canada. Politics is dominated by middle-class males. Large segments of the population remain outside the political process. Mishler has pointed out that lawyers, doctors, businesspeople and other professionals comprise less than 10% of the Canadian workforce but almost 75% of the membership of the House of Commons and of local party organizations. As a result, political decision-making is in the hands of those who are by and large satisfied with the *status quo* (Mishler, 1979).

This state of affairs is neither just nor democratic, and if it is to change, as it must, the schools have their part to play. We must reorient them from their largely conservative role to one which sees them committed to the achievement of social justice and democracy. They must be organized to show students the world as it is, to show them also how it might be, and to give them the knowledge, skills and dispositions to transform one into the other.

We do not know how effective the schools can be in doing this, and it is obvious that at best there are limits to what they can do, but there is room for them to do something. There have always been schools and teachers who have successfully rejected the conservative role assigned to them. Their example points to what is possible.

Chapter Two

SOME RECENT PEDAGOGIES

Although there has not been much public discussion of pedagogy, we do not have to start from scratch. There is a substantial body of work on which to draw, and much of it has considerable relevance to any attempt to connect pedagogy and citizenship. In this context, three pedagogical approaches are of particular interest. They are (1) discovery and inquiry; (2) critical pedagogy; and (3) feminist pedagogy. All emphasize the importance of thinking for oneself, of critical and reflective inquiry, which forms one crucial element of democratic citizenship. At the same time, they take into account the social dimension of citizenship, linking critical, independent thinking, with a concern for participation in the affairs of society in order to achieve the democratic ideals of freedom and justice.

Teaching As Inquiry And Discovery

The traditional view of teaching sees it as the transmission of knowledge and skills, a one-way sending of a message from expert to novice, in which the receiver's job is to take in the message as accurately as possible, without distortion or alteration. In this view teachers are seen as people with special knowledge, skills and expertise, whether gained from experience or from special training, whose task it is to transmit what they know to whoever needs to receive it.

For most of human history, this meant that teachers worked with private students. Though sometimes subject to public regulation, they were essentially free agents, depending on their ability to attract students. With the creation of state education, prescribed curricula and compulsory attendance, teachers became public officials, responsible for knowing and teaching officially controlled knowledge. There were things that students were supposed to know and to do, and that teachers were therefore expected to teach. The creation of state-controlled education thus reinforced a view of teaching that was already sanctioned by over two thousand years of tradition: teaching as transmission. The analogies that have been most often employed to illustrate this conception of teaching have portrayed students as clean slates or empty containers. The teachers' task is to inscribe on the students those things that are thought to be good for them, or to fill the containers with the approved contents.

The transmission view of education obviously vests enormous authority and power in teachers. They have authority, since they are supposed to possess superior knowledge and wisdom that is respected either for its inherent value and status, or because it is officially sanctioned. They have power because they are legally entrusted with the right to train, discipline and punish the young. Conversely, students have neither rights nor power. Their position is in all respects a subordinate one.

Not only does transmission pedagogy assign one particular role to teachers — active, dominant, powerful — and another to students — subordinate, docile, powerless — but it also takes a particular view of curriculum. It sees the curriculum as that which students have to learn, with no if's or but's. The curriculum is vested with a particular authority, and indeed in public school systems it is given legal standing, so that a teacher can be punished for not following it. Ideally, the curriculum represents "the best that has been known and thought," to use Matthew Arnold's nineteenth century phrase, and is therefore worth knowing for its own sake. More often it represents knowledge that is officially declared to be useful and socially necessary. In either case, the curriculum stands external to students' interests and concerns. The task of the student is to learn it, which eventually means to memorize it, and to be tested on it. It is not coincidental that the very word, curriculum, comes from a Latin origin which means a race-course: it is something to be covered.

From the very beginning, there has been an alternative to transmission pedagogy, an alternative that takes a very different view of the role of the teacher, the student and the curriculum. In recent years, it has most commonly gone under the name of inquiry and discovery teaching and learning. A distinction is sometimes made between inquiry and discovery, with the former assigning a more active role to teachers as organizers and shapers of students' learning, and the latter giving more power to students to take the process of discovery wherever it leads. In what follows, however, the two words will be used interchangeably.

At its most basic, this approach to pedagogy says the teacher's task is to stimulate, encourage and guide students, not to memorize what the teacher already knows or what is contained in the curriculum, but to discover it for themselves, through a process of inquiry. Thus, students are required not merely to remember what they have been told, but to investigate, to inquire, to think for themselves. They are seen not as blank slates or empty vessels, but as people who already know a good deal, who in fact know more than they themselves realize. Thus the teacher is there not to fill in the blanks of students' minds, but to use and build on their existing knowledge in order to help them refine and extend that knowledge.

Although it has never been as popular as transmission pedagogy, the discovery and inquiry approach has equally long roots, stretching back at least to Socrates, who insisted that learning meant not stocking the mind with information but thinking through what one already knew, applying it to new situations and, in tackling the problems that arose, extending it and learning more. As Abelard put it in the twelfth century, "careful and frequent questioning is the basic key to wisdom." (Knowles, 1962:125) In this context, the teacher-student relationship becomes not a one-way transmission, but an interaction. Socratic learning cannot take place in isolation or in silence but only in discussion with others, through a process of mutual criticism.

We should keep in mind that Socrates and Abelard were concerned with only one form of knowledge, namely the establishment of water-tight, universal definitions, of such concepts as justice, virtue or piety. Such an undertaking lends itself to the Socratic approach of questioning, criticism, and conceptual analysis, but is not so suitable for the acquisition of empirical, factual knowledge in such subjects as science or history. Nor is the Socratic method necessarily as praiseworthy as its defenders have claimed. Despite Socrates' constant insistence that he knew as little as, and indeed less than, anyone and had therefore no particular goal in view (except conceptual clarity) when he entered into discussion, it is difficult to avoid the impression that his detachment was not innocent. There is something quite unpleasant in his non-stop probing of others' attempted definitions without ever attempting a definition himself. The Socratic method is relentlessly negative, and, when rigorously applied to school-age children (which it rarely is), is clearly damaging. It is far more likely to silence students or convert them to cynicism than to lead them in pursuit of serious knowledge.

Nonetheless, Socrates remains important as a representative of a pedagogy that offers a distinct alternative to the transmission model. Where he led, others followed. The inquiry tradition has been maintained in education, as every age has witnessed those who questioned the dominant tradition and who stressed the power of critical thought.

Perhaps the greatest boost to the pedagogy of discovery and inquiry came with the Scientific Revolution of the seventeenth century. Until then, the quest for knowledge was essentially backward-looking. In the words of Erasmus, the sixteenth-century humanist, all that was worth knowing was to be found in the literature of Greece and Rome. Some would have added the Bible to the list, but the point was that knowledge was finite: all that was worth knowing had already been discovered. The chief intellectual tasks therefore were to understand and preserve it. Hence, for example the lecture, which in its Latin origin, literally means reading. The lecture originated in a pre-print age, when manuscript texts were scarce and expensive. The task of the lecturer, was to read a text to students and to clarify it, by explaining its grammar, its surface meaning and its deeper, less obvious implications. In the whole process, memorization was central. Lecturer and students used mnemonics, question and answer summaries and all kinds of memory-aids. Their shared purpose was to gain command of a set body of knowledge. This, of course, did not preclude approaching the stock of knowledge in a critical spirit, looking for inconsistencies and contradictions and posing difficult questions. Nonetheless, fundamentally, learning meant becoming familiar with an existing tradition.

All this began to change with the Scientific Revolution. An empirical study of anatomy and other natural phenomena showed the Latin and Greek authorities to be wrong. Questions were posed for which the ancient learning had no answer. Knowledge was to be discovered not through pondering the classics, but through observation and experiment. As the Puritan John Webster wrote in 1653, knowledge and understanding were the result of "... true and infallible demonstration, observation and experiment, the only certain means to discover and anatomize nature's occult and central operations; which are found out by laborious trials, manual operations, assiduous observations and the like, and not by boring continually upon a few paper idols and unexperienced authors." (Webster, 1653:68) And unlike the classical tradition, scientific learning was not finite. It continually expanded, making it ever more difficult for an educated person to know all that was worth knowing.

The Scientific Revolution thus reinforced the pedagogical tradition that emphasized inquiry and discovery while also giving it a new direction. The tradition had always had its defenders, but of necessity they had worked with words and texts. Their approach to inquiry was above all verbal and placed a heavy emphasis on dialectic, on logic. The Scientific Revolution turned instead not to words but to things. Logic and purely verbal argument were put aside. John Webster rejected them as "... a civil war of words, a verbal contest, a combat of winning craftiness," characterized by "... independence, insolence, opposition, contradiction, derision, diversion, trifling, jeering, humming, hissing, brawling, quarrelling, scolding, scandalizing, and the like" (Webster, 1653:33).

Webster was a controversialist and presented his arguments in extreme terms, but in essence his views were shared by most of the champions of the new science. The pedagogical implications were obvious and were most clearly drawn by the seventeenth century Czech educational theorist, Comenius. He rejected the traditional emphasis on words and texts, which were generally pitched at a level beyond students' understanding and thus compelled a reliance on rote memory and coercive discipline. Instead he insisted on the importance of the senses, and especially of observation, of the use of pictures and objects, and of the value of the child's own ideas. As he put it: "Men (*sic*) must, as far as possible, be taught to become wise by studying the heavens, the earth, oaks and beeches, but not by studying books: that is to say, they must learn to know and investigate the things themselves, and not the observations that other people have made about the things...." He went on to make a general rule: "... no information should be imparted on the grounds of bookish authority, but should be authorized by actual demonstration for the senses and to the intellect" (Rusk, 1957:95).

This approach to pedagogy had obvious consequences for the roles of teachers and students. It drastically reduced the importance of transmission, and put much greater emphasis on students' own ideas and contributions. Ideally, this meant that teachers would rely less on power and punishment and more on trust and cooperation. In Comenius' words: "Let the main object of our Didactic be... to seek and find a method of instruction by which our teachers may teach less, but learners may learn more, by which schools may be the scene of less noise, aversion and useless labour, but of more leisure, enjoyment and solid progress" (Eby, 1952:200).

The seventeenth century, then, saw the development of a pedagogy of inquiry and discovery (though these words were not used at the time), based upon observation and experiment, and upon a view of children as active learners whose knowledge and experience were to be respected and extended. This pedagogy was further developed in the eighteenth century under the influence of the Enlightenment, with its faith in human progress and the power of reason. The rationalism of the Enlightenment provoked the reaction of Romanticism, with its emphasis on the emotions and instinct, but the Romantics, with their belief in authentic human response, also valued the experience of childhood and thus favoured a pedagogy that made teaching subordinate to the needs of children. When Froebel opened his first kindergarten in 1837, the name was carefully chosen. It was a garden for children, who were seen not as clean slates or empty pitchers, but as plants who contained within themselves the potential for fruitful growth.

Both the Enlightenment and Romanticism valued a child-centred pedagogy. One emphasized reason, the other the emotions, but both rejected any view of pedagogy as transmission: "I hate books," wrote Rousseau in 1762, "they merely teach us to talk of what we do not know." Or again, "Things! Things! I shall never repeat often enough that we give too much power to words. With our babbling education we make nothing but babblers" (Rousseau, 1762:143). Children learn through activity in confronting problems that they must use their experience and their reason to solve. If, for example, teachers want to teach children some basic geographic concepts, they should not do so from books. They should take their students out into the world and let them observe and hypothesize. They should not learn maps but make them, or, rather, they should learn them by making them. They should be taken out so that they lose their way in the forest, if necessary, so that they will have to learn how to find their way home. "My purpose," wrote Rousseau of his imaginary pupil Émile, "is not at all to give him knowledge but to teach him how to acquire it when necessary..." (Eby, 1952:356). Pestalozzi made a similar point: "It is a principle of ours that the teacher should aim rather at increasing the powers of his pupil than at increasing his (*sic*) knowledge" (Eby, 1952:426). It is, of course, true that Rousseau and others saw this kind of education as necessary only for boys. For Rousseau, in particular, the education of girls was to be designed to make them useful and pleasing to men. But this is a fault in Rousseau, not in his pedagogy. Discovery and inquiry are obviously equally suitable to girls and boys and, indeed, Rousseau's reasons for distinguishing the sexes derived not from any pedagogical principle but from his social and political theory.

It should not be thought, however, that the new pedagogy carried all before it. Galiéni's response to Rousseau has already been mentioned. Above all, the state systems of public schooling that were created in the nineteenth century were, for the most part, opposed to the pedagogy of discovery and inquiry. Schools were intended not to educate children but to train them: to turn them into loyal, obedient national citizens with approved knowledge and values. Schools were intended not for the welfare of children but the good of the state.

Not that schools were ever so monolithic that they could exclude all rivals to transmission pedagogy. There were always teachers and administrators who rejected it, and there were from time to time reform movements that attempted to give official sanction to discovery and inquiry.

Discovery and inquiry have thus found a place in the schools. Though practised in only a minority of classrooms, they are present to a greater extent than ever before. Their legitimacy, however, can never be taken for granted and it is helpful for anyone committed to them to know something of their history and tradition, which has been very briefly sketched here.

The two names most often associated with inquiry and discovery in our century are those of John Dewey and Jerome Bruner. Dewey built upon the tradition of earlier educational reformers, running back to Pestalozzi and Rousseau and anticipating the "natural method" promoted by Célestin Freinet. Like them, he insisted that education had to be appropriate to children's levels of development, to their abilities and needs, and that pedagogy must provide children with the opportunity for experience and observation. In his view, learning arises from activity and problem-solving and pedagogy must provide children with both. School subjects or academic disciplines, as traditionally defined, should not be directly taught. For Dewey, the disciplines represented the sum of adult experience and, as such, were incomprehensible to children, who could learn them only by rote, without understanding, and without any opportunity for growth to occur. And for Dewey, human growth, the achievement of potential, was the central purpose of education. Education for growth was the best training for citizenship, especially in a democracy. Growth, in Dewey's sense of the word, meant that men and women would be empowered to act in society in ways that would involve them cooperatively with others.

In all this, pedagogy was assigned a central role, and it was a pedagogy of discovery and inquiry. For Dewey, learning occurs when one meets a problem that needs solving, and it occurs most effectively when one can arrive at and test a range of solutions in consultation with others. Thus, pedagogy must arrange for problems that are meaningful to students, that call for cooperative action, and that stimulate growth and development. Dewey's description of the teaching of geography provides a helpful example of what this could mean in practice. He described the experience of seven-year old students in his Laboratory School at the University of Chicago. The students were interested in what Dewey called "the typical activities of primitive peoples." Here, then, was the germ of the problem that could become the basis for teaching. The students had an interest, and the pedagogical question thus became, "... what are we to do with this interest — are we to ignore it, or just excite and draw it out? Or shall we get hold of it and direct it to something ahead, something better?" Dewey made clear his preference for the last, thus reminding us that "discovery" learning does not free the teacher from responsibility. Instead, it makes the teacher responsible for ensuring that what is discovered is educationally valuable.

In this case, the teacher began by getting the children to imagine themselves living in early times, in direct contact with nature. They speculated about living in caves or trees, depending on hunting and fishing. They went on to imagine life in different stages of history: hunting, nomadic, agricultural. All this provided a base for and a point of contact with knowledge: "The point I wish to make", wrote Dewey, "is that there is abundant opportunity thus given for actual study, for inquiry which results in gaining information." In other words, discovery learning does not exclude the use of more conventional forms of teaching; rather it provides a way of making it more effective, since students acquire information in response to a felt need and a sense of problem. Further, the whole exercise provides an opportunity for more concrete, hands-on activity. "For example, the children had some idea of primitive weapons, of the stone arrowhead, etc. That provided occasion for the testing of materials as regards their viability, their shape, texture, etc., resulting in a lesson in mineralogy, as they examined the different stones to find what was best suited to their purpose." Similarly, discussion of the iron age led to experiments with the construction of a smelting-oven with much use of trial and error. The children did experiments with other metals also. All this led to geography, with the children discussing what physical conditions would best support the forms of life and what methods of exchange would exist. "Having worked out such points in conversation, they (i.e., students) have afterward represented them in maps and sand-molding." Throughout, notes Dewey, "the instruction was not given ready-made; it was first needed, and then arrived at experimentally."

As to the overall value of the pedagogical approach, Dewey was emphatic: "The result, to my mind, justifies completely the conviction that children, in a year of such work (of five hours a week altogether), get infinitely more acquaintance with facts of science, geography, and anthropology than they get where information is the professed end and object, where they are simply set to learning facts in fixed lessons. As to discipline, they get more training in attention, more power of interpretation, of drawing inferences, of acute observation and continuous reflection, than if they were put to working out arbitrary problems simply for the sake of discipline" (Dewey, 1899/1956:53-54).

In addition, this pedagogical approach lent itself to teaching students a problem-solving method capable of general application, both inside and outside school. In *How We Think*, Dewey provided such a method, consisting essentially of these five steps:

1. Recognizing that a problem exists.
2. Defining the exact nature of the problem.
3. Formulating possible solutions.
4. Testing the most likely solutions.
5. Arriving at the most satisfactory solution.

Such a method of analysis was not only a useful educational tool, it was also in Dewey's view an indispensable ingredient of democratic citizenship.

To be successful, Dewey's pedagogy demands a very high level of skill on the part of teachers, who must not only have a rich general knowledge and social awareness, but also an ability to assess students' needs and abilities and to design instruction accordingly. It is more difficult to do properly than transmission pedagogy and places much greater demands on the teacher. Perhaps not surprisingly, and despite popular mythology, Dewey had little real influence on most schools, which either carried on unchanged in their attachment to transmission pedagogy, or misunderstood his message and resorted to an unthinking reliance of student activity for its own sake, regardless of underlying purpose. One of the strongest pedagogical movements to promote this approach to problem solving has been *La Pédagogie Freinet*, a co–operative organization founded and inspired by the French elementary school teacher, Célistin Freinet (1896-1966). Spreading from France throughout mainland Europe and beyond from the 1930s on, it combined co–operative learning techniques with a Dewey–like insistence on inquiry and discovery.

Discovery and inquiry achieved a new lease of life throughout the English–speaking world in the 1960's, especially after the 1963 appearance of Jerome Bruner's *The Process of Education* and its argument that discovery learning was both the most natural and the most effective way for students to learn. Bruner argued that it would make possible the transfer of learning from subject to subject, as students learned the skills and dispositions needed for problem-solving. It would reduce the gap between the kinds of thinking done by students and those done by scholars. It would form the best introduction to the various subjects by teaching their central ways of thinking. It would make learning more interesting and thus provide its own motivation. And it would make schools centres of intellectual excitement.

Bruner, a prominent Harvard psychologist, was critical of existing pedagogy, which he saw as boring and destructive of students' potential. In his words: "Young children in school expend extraordinary time and effort figuring out what it is that the teacher wants — and usually coming to the conclusion that she or he wants tidiness or remembering or doing things at a certain time in a certain way." (Bruner, 1971:62) His condemnation of geography textbooks can be taken as representative of his view of all aspects of school curricula and materials, and the pedagogy associated with them:

> Find if you can any similarity between geography as presented in the usual textbook and geography as practised by geographers. The problems are presented as solved at the outset. The child is then asked to consider how the "authority" arrived at his solution. In a geography text we will find at the beginning of a chapter the statement, "The world can be divided into temperate, torrid, and frigid zones." Virtually the whole of the effort in the paragraphs that follow is given over to making it seem as if this distinction is obvious. Many children, we are convinced, are left with an image of an earth in which one can find border signs which read something of the order, "You are now entering the temperate zone," put there by some benign authority in league with the textbook writer. The problem, how to characterize the surface of the earth in terms of regions, disappears and geography is converted into a combination of tongue-twisting names in a gazetteer and some rather puzzling maps in which "Greenland looks much bigger than it is." What is lost in this arbitrariness is a development of a sense of problem in the child. (Bruner, 1971:92)

As an alternative to this one-way transmission of information with which students could make little or no personal connection, Bruner offered a pedagogy based upon discovery. In his approach, students are faced with a problem, wherever possible presented through stimulating materials. The problem is pitched at a level that makes it neither too difficult to solve nor too easy. As Dewey had noted: "A large part of the art of instruction lies in making the difficulty of new problems large enough to challenge thought, and small enough so that... there shall be luminous familiar spots from which helpful suggestions may spring" (Dewey, 1916:157). Above all, problems must require students to draw upon what they already know, to apply it in a new situation, and in so doing extend it further. As Bruner said: "Learning is, most often, figuring out how to use what you already know in order to go beyond what you currently think" (Bruner, 1983:183). Students were also encouraged to think, to guess, to speculate, to bounce ideas off each other, to develop confidence in their ability to use their minds. In Bruner's words, "Children, like adults, need reassurance that it is all right to entertain and express highly subjective ideas, to treat a task as a problem where you *invent* an answer rather than *finding* one out there in the book or on the blackboard" (Bruner, 1971:62).

As an example of how this pedagogy actually works in the classroom, Bruner described a Grade 6 geography class studying the north-eastern United States. Instead of presenting the students with all the necessary facts, the teacher gave them an outline map indicating physical features and resources and asked them where they thought that people would settle. In the process of generating their answers, the students provided a wealth of hypotheses and arguments, not only solving the problem they had been set but also generating a high level of interest and of confidence in themselves. The lesson nicely illustrates Bruner's point that "... discovery teaching generally involves not so much the process of leading students to discover what is 'out there' but, instead their discovering what is in their own heads. It involves encouraging them to say, let me stop and think about that; let me use my head; let me have some vicarious trial-and-error" (Bruner, 1971:72). This same approach can be seen in another example, this time involving language. In this instance, the teacher wrote a simple sentence on the board, of the nature of "the man ate his lunch." Students were asked to make some similar sentences, so that something like this appeared:

The	man	ate	his	lunch.
A	boy	stole	a	bike.
The	dog	chased	my	cat.
My	father	skidded	the	car.
A	wind	blew	his	hat.

Students can make up as many sentences as they wish, but at some point the teacher presents them with a puzzle: how is that one can go from left to right, choosing words from any row, and still end up with a grammatically correct sentence, although it may have a nonsensical meaning, e.g., "The dog ate my car"? Once they have explored this concept, students were asked if they could make up more columns, using adjectives and adverbs, for example. They did and, in Bruner's words, "... they were ready and willing now to get into the syntax of the language to invent it afresh" (Bruner, 1971:74). In doing so, they were also ready to consider new ideas and terminology introduced by the teacher.

The approach is easily applied to all subjects in the curriculum and Dewey summarized it in this way: "... first, that the pupil have a genuine situation of experience... that there be a continuous activity in which he (*sic*) is interested for its own sake; secondly, that a genuine problem develop within this situation as a stimulus to thought; third, that he possess the information and make the observations needed to deal with it; fourth, that suggested solutions occur to him which he shall be responsible for developing in an orderly way; fifth, that he have opportunity and occasion to test his ideas by application, to make their meaning clear, and to discover for himself their validity" (Dewey, 1916/1966:163).

Using this as a basis, and adding to it contributions from other theorists and researchers, it is possible to identify the following six components of discovery-inquiry pedagogy.

1. Teaching And Learning Are Based Upon Problems

The first step is to organize what is to be learned as a problem for students to tackle. Learning must appear not as something simply to be done as a classroom exercise, but as something that students consider meaningful and interesting. This will occur only if it speaks to their own concerns or because it has been made real by stimulating teaching. It is obviously very easy to design problems that are no more than busy-work or that are seen by students as totally pointless. It is crucial, therefore, to work with problems that students find meaningful. It is also important to see that problems are pitched at the right level of difficulty, being neither too simple nor too difficult. Students should be able to tackle them by drawing on their previous experience and knowledge but in ways that lead them to think in new ways about what they already know.

2. Students Must Be Aware Of Techniques of Thinking

Students must realize that learning means thinking, not just memorizing, and that thinking means feeling free to take risks. Thinking can be rather like speaking a foreign language, where it can happen that people know a language but lack confidence in their ability to speak it. It is the same with thinking. Teachers must therefore do everything that they can to show students that thinking is encouraged, welcomed and indeed demanded. Classroom posters, codes of conduct, letters to parents, statements of school goals, course objectives, the nature of assignments, teachers' own behaviour — all should demonstrate the central role of thinking.

Moreover, students should be explicitly taught how to think. They must learn to think about thinking, to apply explicit models of critical thinking, problem–solving, decision-making and other forms of thinking. This is not to suggest that effective thinking can be reduced to a formula, but formulas can be helpful guides to thinking, especially for students. Recent writers have provided a variety of models of thinking, designed to be taught to students (Ennis, 1962; Fenton, 1968; de Bono, 1982; Beyer, 1988; Siegel, 1988; Paul, 1989). There is not space to examine them here, but they can make an important contribution to discovery and inquiry.

3. Student Participation

Discovery-inquiry obviously depends upon a high degree of student participation and this is largely a function of classroom climate. The evidence is conclusive that in many classrooms students are passive. Their tasks are to copy work from the board or overhead, to complete worksheets, to respond to teachers' questions. Obviously this pattern must change. More use must be made of experiential learning, whether through role-playing, simulation, discussion or some other form. Students must feel a sense of ownership of their classrooms, so that they feel free to act naturally in them. They must see the point and relevance of what they are being asked to do, and they should have a voice in deciding what this is.

4. The Role Of Discussion And Dialogue

Discovery-inquiry is much more a collective than an individual affair. Obviously, an individual can pursue inquiry alone, but at some point the results of this inquiry have to be communicated to others. More important, in a classroom, inquiry works best when students work together, sharing ideas, generating hypotheses, offering criticism and advice. In all of this, discussion is fundamental. As with thinking, two conditions are necessary: first, students must possess the necessary skills, and second, they must be willing to use them. Discussion, in other words, must be explicitly taught if it is to be more than merely shouting down one's opponents. It must be seen not as a win-or-lose debate, but as a dialogue in which people collaborate to explore matters of common interest. The pedagogy of discussion is discussed in more detail in Chapter 4, but it is obviously fundamental to discovery and inquiry.

5. The Provision Of Appropriate Materials

Discovery and inquiry cannot take place in a vacuum. At some point, once students have begun to explore a problem, they will need information if they are to test ideas, to generate hypotheses, to pursue useful leads. The discovery-inquiry classroom needs more resources, or at least access to more resources (books, videos, experts, magazines, etc.) than its conventional counterpart. Transmission pedagogy can survive with one teacher and one textbook; discovery and inquiry cannot. At the same time, it is obviously important that the resources are such that students can use and understand them. This does not mean that we must become the slaves of reading formulas and other alleged indicators of usefulness, for when students become intrigued by a problem there is often no limit to what they can read and understand. It does mean that we should make available to students a wide range and variety of resources. There is no reason, for example, why each classroom should not have its own system of files of useful material, taken from newspapers, magazines and similar sources. Much can be done by students themselves to help collect the resources upon which discovery-inquiry depends. Parents, the community, labour and business, interest groups, government agencies, the media — all are sources of useful material.

6. The Role of the Teacher

Though discovery-inquiry pedagogy changes the roles of teachers and students and makes students more active participants in their own learning, teachers are no less active than in the transmission model. They might instruct less; but they teach more, for inquiry demands a good deal of preparation if students are to handle it successfully. Throughout his life, Dewey protested against the misapplication of his method by teachers who believed that all they had to do was to turn children loose on some activity. As he put it: "The belief that all genuine education comes about through experience does not mean that all experiences are genuinely or equally educative" (Dewey, 1938/1963:25).

Discovery-inquiry sees an active role for teachers in organizing materials and experiences so that students are faced with problems; so that students feel confident in their ability to think and to work together; so that they have the skills and attitudes that make discovery-inquiry successful; so that they find the materials they need to pursue their inquiries; so that they experience challenge and success. It has been said that discovery-inquiry makes teachers more stage-managers than actors, but they are no less busy for that. Indeed, discovery-inquiry makes far larger organizational demands upon teachers than does transmission pedagogy, which is no doubt a partial explanation of why it is much less widespread in classrooms.

An example might help to clarify what is involved in discovery-inquiry. In the late 1960's, Hodgetts examined the teaching of Canadian history in schools. For the most part, he saw little of value happening, but this is what he had to say about the classrooms that impressed him (Hodgetts, 1968:54-56).

First, the students were well prepared. The reading assignments given to them had been planned carefully and the source material to which they had been guided introduced controversial, opposing or supplementary viewpoints. In addition, the readings gave additional factual material from which the students themselves developed different viewpoints. The outstanding feature of all these classes, however, was the almost total absence of any factual recall techniques. There was no lecturing by the teacher; no factual question-answer period to see what the class had remembered; the students did not read their reports aloud to each other. The teacher assumed that students had mastered most of the factual information for themselves and that any misunderstandings would be clarified in using the facts rather than in hammering them home through recitation. Students were expected to advance viewpoints, defend positions with evidence, and develop general concepts. Thus the entire lesson revolved around a discussion of ideas — but, ideas that the teacher, or frequently the students themselves, insisted should be supported by relevant factual information.

Second, the students had developed or were in the process of developing remarkable skill in discussion techniques. They did most of the talking. Frequently they spoke back and forth to each other and became so absorbed in what they were doing that the presence of the teacher temporarily faded into the background. They had been taught to respect each other's points of view, to keep an open mind and to listen to evidence from other sources. Consequently, there was a genuine exchange of ideas, a true dialogue.

Third, none of these classes was completely student-centred. At times, teachers intervened either to being the class back on topic, to correct an obvious error in fact, or to express their own ideas. The success of the classes was partly dependent on the fact that teachers themselves were interested and competent in what they were teaching. They were neither grayed-out neutrals nor domineering masters. They used good discussion techniques and, by example, enhanced this quality in their students. They communicated well with their students and had their respect and confidence.

Fourth, without exception, classes were studying a topic in depth, not as a change of pace but as a regular practice. This was apparent in the wording of the topic (usually phrased to pose a question, a controversial set of viewpoints or a "problem" to be solved), in the nature of the reading assignments, in the depth of discussion, and in the type of notebooks kept by the students. Textbooks may or may not have been used as a basic starting point, but there was an air of interest and expectation that motivated the students to travel far beyond the textbook. The topics were so rich and the discussions so good that virtually all of these lessons spilled over from the one class period to another.

Fifth, these classes emphasized the development of intellectual abilities. By their very nature, they provided the opportunity and the incentive for students to think for themselves; to make the factual evidence work for them; to weigh and evaluate evidence; to increase their powers of oral and written expression. Hodgetts saw the implication of this for citizenship, noting that "It is generally agreed that intellectual skills like these have a transfer value to them into life situations. As an independent decision-maker in all levels of society, facing complex, rapidly changing situations, the citizen in a democracy needs the tools (as distinct from the knowledge) to make these decisions effectively." He makes here too great a distinction between skills and knowledge, and dismisses knowledge too easily, but it is certainly true that we must not neglect to include skills as part of our teaching.

Finally, it is worth noting that these classes were not confined to the so-called top or best students. Hodgetts made a point of noting that he found them across the range of academic and ability levels, observing that slightly less than half of the total were "specially selected, above average" classes. In fact, his conclusions are worth emphasizing. His observations in classrooms across the country convinced him that so-called student ability was not a determining factor in using inquiry techniques. He urged teachers to abandon their conventional wisdom about difficult classes: "As long as the students in this type of class are taught by hastily designed, dull, exposition methods based on the assumption that 'you can't do much with these kids anyway,' they will continue to be unmotivated, uninterested, and difficult." Inquiry teaching, he insisted, works with all students, not only with the academic minority. (Hodgetts, 1968:56)

Critical Pedagogy

Critical pedagogy rose to prominence in the 1980's. It is both an extension of and a reaction to the Marxist analyses of education that appeared in preceding years, highlighted by the appearance in 1976 of Bowles and Gintis' *Schooling in Capitalist America* and Roger Dale's British collection, *Schooling and Capitalism.* Closer to home, two influential Marxist analyses had already been published in Quebec by the province's teachers' union (CEQ): *L'école au service de la classe dominante* (1972) and *Le manuel du premier mai* (1975).

In essence, critical pedagogy accepts the main points of the Marxist critique of schooling, but at the same time points to their limitations and goes beyond them. It draws not only upon Marxist but upon literary theory, feminism, liberation theology, critical theory, and a variety of other sources.

It seems best to begin by looking briefly at the main elements of the Marxist analysis of education. It should be emphasized at the outset that there is no one unified Marxist theory of education. There is a good deal of disagreement and mutual criticism among Marxists.

The most fundamental feature of the Marxist analysis of education is its placement of schooling in its full social context. Schools are not seen in a vacuum, but as existing with other institutions in a social setting, full of economic, political and cultural meanings. This is itself a refreshing change from the majority of educational discussion that treats schools in more or less total isolation, except for such phrases as "society expects" or "the needs of society", that hide more than they reveal. Who, after all, speaks for society? Who determines what it needs? Whose view of society is being given pride of place? Is society really so unified and consensual? Marxist analysis gives these questions a central place, insisting that in a society characterized by political and economic inequality schooling plays a key role in maintaining and legitimizing that inequality. It sees the educational system as a sorting machine, selecting youngsters for different slots in the economic and political system. Some do not complete high school; some end their formal education with a high school diploma; others go on to college or university, and even to graduate school. In one sense this is not especially controversial. Much allegedly common-sense thinking assumes that this sorting out of students is both necessary and inevitable; necessary because the economic system depends upon people having different skills, inevitable because, it is claimed, different students have different levels of ability and intelligence and, therefore, cannot all equally profit from education.

Marxists, and socialists generally, reject this argument. They point to the evidence indicating that students are assigned to differing levels of education not by ability but by social class; or, more subtly, that the particular definition of ability that schools use works to the disadvantage of large groups of students. Thus, middle–class children are more likely to be found in academic programs in high school and to go on to university than are working class children. Moreover, this provision of unequal education is neither accidental nor the apparently natural result of children's differing abilities; it is a necessary and integral feature of a capitalist economy that depends upon a labour force of differing levels of skill, ranging from executives through administrators to workers, be they skilled, semi-skilled or unskilled, all with differing amounts of power, influence and wealth.

This system of structured inequality is integral to capitalism, and its strength and stability rest upon the fact that most people see it as natural and inevitable. The victims of the system tend to blame not the system for its inequalities, but themselves for their failure to "make it." In this way, the dominant groups in society maintain their hegemony. They do not have to use coercion or physical force. They persuade those they dominate that this is simply the way the world works. Indeed, they probably believe it quite sincerely. As a result, awkward questions are not asked. The *status quo* is maintained.

In other words, there is a cultural as well as an economic dimension to what schools do. Different levels of education provide different levels of access to knowledge by maintaining different curricula: university entrance, advanced placement, general, commercial, vocational, and the rest. Given the reality that different kinds of knowledge enjoy different levels of status and prestige, and therefore confer or deny particular social benefits, students are thus further sorted. Moreover, schooling works in ways that make this sorting appear natural and objective so that when students are placed in dead-end or low-status programs it is made to seem that this is the unavoidable result of their lack of ability. Indeed, it is usually presented as being in their best interest, since to put them in an academic program would only expose them to frustration and failure. These distinctions are further reinforced by teachers, who teach different levels of students in different ways, so that "bright" students receive more stimulating teaching, while "slower" students are taught in more routine, pedestrian ways since this is all they are thought capable of handling. In schools, as elsewhere, the more you have, the more you get. In the process, students themselves usually come to accept as valid the verdict passed on to them by their schools, leading, in the case of students who do not do well, either to a sense of failure and inadequacy or a rejection of all that school has to offer — or both.

The Marxist term for this whole process — here drastically simplified — is reproduction. The argument is that any social system has not only to produce the material goods it needs for survival, but also to reproduce the conditions necessary for its continuing existence, including the kinds of knowledge, skills, attitudes and values upon which the system depends. In a society in which inequalities exist, and that depends on their existence for its survival, education plays a major role in determining who gets what, and, equally important, in ensuring that the fundamental inequalities are seen as fair and reasonable. The French Marxist, Louis Althusser, for example, described schooling as a crucial part of what he called the Ideological State Apparatus, the machinery of state that serves not to coerce people physically but to persuade them, without their even realizing, that they live in the best of all possible worlds.

In some Marxist analysis, social reproduction works in another way also, through what has been called the correspondence principle. In this analysis, schools serve to prepare students for different kinds of work and social roles, and therefore for different and unequal access to power and influence, not simply by what and how they teach, but by embodying in their very operation the principles of different kinds of workplace. Schools which send many students on to university and thus on to professional and executive careers — in other words, largely suburban, middle–class, academic schools — build into their operating methods principles of autonomy, independence, student participation in decision-making. Conversely, schools that send their students straight to the labour market where they will hold largely semi-skilled or unskilled jobs, emphasize obedience, routine, conformity to rules. There is, in other words, a direct correspondence between school and workplace.

This, in barest outline, is the Marxist analysis of schooling. Its three central concepts are hegemony, reproduction and correspondence. Behind these are the familiar Marxist analytical tools of social class, ideology and capital. In the Marxist view, schools are neither innocent nor neutral. They were created to sustain and legitimize a particular social order, and they reflect and maintain the characteristics of that order. In a capitalist society, schools prepare students for capitalism. And though Marxism traditionally sees the world in terms of social class, this general analysis can also be applied to matters of gender and race. The cultural assumptions of schools, the biases of textbooks and curricula, the attitudes and actions of teachers and others, can all serve to sort students by race and ethnic background and by gender, as well as by social class.

Critical pedagogy accepts much of this analysis, but criticizes Marxism for not taking it far enough and for applying it too rigidly. It rightly accuses Marxism (at least in some of its versions) of leaving no room whatsoever for human action, of portraying teachers and students as either dupes or victims of the system, unwilling or powerless to counteract it. In this connection, Marxism also assumes too close a link between education and the imperatives of the economic order and the state system that sustains it. In its most rigid form, Marxism sees education as part of the social "superstructure" which is shaped by economic forces. In short, Marxists are accused of not allowing for contradictions in the system, of not seeing the room for manœuvre that exists in schools, of failing to recognize that meanings and interpretations are not simply imposed on people but rather are constructed by them. Marxism has stressed the structure of the social and educational system and the constraints it places on people, but in so doing, it has denied or underestimated the scope and power of human agency, of the ability of people to resist and even transform the structure within which they live. This tendency in Marxism has led it to take a very pessimistic view of the possibility of change through education. If schooling is determined by economic and political imperatives, then presumably it will change only when economic and political changes occur. Thus, Harris concludes that "... the basic schooling process cannot be fundamentally changed independent of changing the mode of production of which that process is an integral part." (Harris, 1982:144)

It should be noted that these criticisms do not apply with equal force to all forms of Marxism, and that they are not as valid today as they were a few years ago. Marxists do now acknowledge the relative autonomy of the school from the economic and political forces that surround it. They no longer see the superstructure as a merely passive reflection of the economic base of society. They do allow for contradiction and resistance in the operation of schooling. They would not disagree with Giroux that schools are "... arenas of contestation and struggle among differentially empowered cultural and economic groups." (Giroux, 1984:3)

What distinguishes critical pedagogy, however, is that it draws from a wider range of sources than Marxism alone, and that it insists upon the possibility, and indeed the practicality of a pedagogy that will contribute to social change. This is the meaning, for example, of Jean Anyon's concept of "transformative pedagogics" — a pedagogy that will transform both the taken-for-granted routines of teaching and learning and the social system of which they are a reflection.

It is true that the exponents of critical pedagogy have dwelt more on the theory of pedagogy than on its practice and that they are too often disposed to neglect the concrete for the abstract. As a result, the writing on critical pedagogy is often unnecessarily obscure and fails to make contact with the people for whom it would be most useful. In some forms, it is more a contribution to social theory than to pedagogy. Nonetheless, it is worth exploring, especially to anyone who wishes to take advantage of the potential of pedagogy for bringing about a genuinely democratic citizenship.

It must be remembered that critical pedagogy, by definition, is not a solidly uniform body of theory. The very word "critical" indicates its commitment to criticism and constant reassessment of its assumptions. Nonetheless, bearing in mind that such a procedure obscures some distinctions and differences, it is possible to outline what teaching would be like if the principles of critical pedagogy were followed.

First, critical pedagogy insists upon the importance of theory and theoretical analysis. In its view, teaching is not simply a technique or a craft; it must be philosophically informed and it must draw its theory not merely from the world of education (for example, as in the case of learning theory), but from the social and political realms also. Whatever their subject or specialty, teachers must realize that all education is political education in that it is intended to give special status to some views of the world and to condemn others, either by negative critique or by simple omission. Teachers must therefore understand the relationships among ideology, power, culture and curriculum. As Roger Simon puts it, they must be able to answer these questions: "What counts as knowledge? How is such knowledge produced and distributed? What concerns do different forms of knowledge and knowledge production address? Whose interests do such forms serve? Whose interests are in opposition to the dominant ideology? Do certain forms of engaging knowledge help to legitimate one set of interests over and above others? How might knowledge be engaged so that alternate forms of knowledge and knowledge production might be considered? Where ultimately will the teacher and student stand regarding the interests which underlie the pursuit of knowledge? Given the pursuit of knowledge, what is to be done" (Simon, 1985:1119)?

These questions could be stated more clearly, but their general drift is clear. They make the point that knowledge is not necessarily objective or neutral. They present an enormous research agenda, involving a thorough exploration of history, sociology, educational theory, political philosophy, cultural studies and on and on. For practical purposes they need further simplification, and perhaps the most useful way to achieve this is to think in terms of the well-known formulation of Raymond Williams, that a curriculum is a selection from the culture. Once this central and fairly straightforward point is grasped, then other questions flow more or less naturally. Who does the selecting? On what criteria? For what purposes? What has been emphasized? What has been omitted? What alternatives exist? In any event, some such list of questions is important so that teachers are constantly examining what and how they are teaching. The important and practical consequences of pursuing questions such as these can easily be seen in recent analyses of history and social studies textbooks and programs, showing how little attention they have paid to the history of women, native people, minorities or working people generally.

There is a second component of this theoretical analysis that critical pedagogy sees as important. It consists of an analysis of the role and functions of schooling. To some extent, this is obviously bound up with the questions that Simon has listed, since one cannot properly consider curriculum, ideology and the rest without paying some attention to the institution of schooling that has been created to instil them. In particular, it means being familiar with the debate that has occurred in recent years in the historiography of schooling and that has moved through a sequence of perspectives. The sequence began with the traditional view of schools as beneficent vehicles of social mobility and intellectual enrichment. It moved on to the more neutral view of schools as agents of socialization and assimilation. Next came more critical views of schools as enforcers of social control, ideology and false consciousness. Finally we reach our current, and surely more satisfactory view, of schools as arenas of conflict where differing agendas meet and which thus contain the possibility of genuinely educational work.

There are, no doubt, other elements of theoretical knowledge that teachers should have: for example, they should know something about the subjects they are planning to teach; they should know something about the psychology of the children whom they teach; and so on. Still, for good and obvious reasons, critical pedagogy has not dwelt on these, since they are firmly established in the mainstream of teacher education, and do not address the specific concerns that are central to critical pedagogy, and specifically its commitments to social and political transformation.

These two elements, then, which might be called simply a theory of culture and a theory of schooling, are crucial to critical pedagogy. The argument is that teachers must have examined and must continually examine the many questions that both theories raise, in order that they understand what they are doing and what they might do.

A third element in critical pedagogy is more explicitly directed to immediate classroom concerns. Critical pedagogy sees and rejects most curricula as alien to students, remote from their own experience, foreign to their culture, and simply imposed upon them. It shares the long tradition in pedagogy that learning must be based on and arise from what students already know.

Critical pedagogy takes this beyond a mere pedagogical device, and insists that any pedagogy that ignores students' experience and culture is not only doomed to failure but, much worse, represents a form of ideological imposition which, in turn, reflects and enhances a particular balance of political and social power. Recently, some have argued for organizing curricula around the experience of popular culture, arguing that student experience is shaped by popular culture and that it can thus serve as an ideal vehicle for the development of critical literacy (Giroux and Simon, 1989). Thus, Giroux argues for a "pedagogical practice that uses the lived experience of students themselves as a starting point for developing classroom experiences in which students discover how they give meaning to the world and how such meaning can be used reflectively to discover its own sources and limits" (Giroux, 1981:29). This is more than a restatement of the obvious point that what we teach must be somehow connected to students' existing knowledge and experience. Critical pedagogy goes far beyond the widely accepted view that teaching which is not so connected is likely to fail. A political point is being made here to the effect that students' knowledge and experience, the way they see the world, should become part of the curriculum itself.

At the same time, critical pedagogy recognizes that students' experience might contain unacceptable values, be they racist, sexist, violent, or whatever. Thus, while using students' experience as a way to open up genuinely educational work, as a way to make students more reflective and thoughtful, and as a way to connect educational activity with worthwhile action for social change (as for example in community education), teachers must also go beyond students' experience at some point in order to introduce students to a wider world of ideas and knowledge. In Giroux's words: "All modes of radical pedagogy presuppose a critical education in which students will be given the opportunity to validate their own experiences... this should be the basis for a more distanced and critically directed mode of pedagogy, one that provides students with access to the dominant discourse, skills and academic traditions" (Giroux, 1981:31).

This concern for students' experience is directly connected with a fourth element of critical pedagogy, concerning the role of the student in the classroom. Critical pedagogy insists upon classrooms that operate on humane and democratic principles, in which there is an open and equal relationship between teachers and students, and in which there is a heavy reliance on discussion and dialogue. Giroux's concept of student "voice" combines both ideas: first, that students' experience is important, should be respected and is of pedagogical value; and second, that classrooms must provide space and opportunity for students' voices to be heard. To put it simply, critical pedagogy, at least in this respect, builds upon that long educational tradition that emphasizes students taking an active part in their own learning, both in the ways in which they learn and in the opportunity to participate in the selection of what is to be learned, and how. For critical pedagogy, active learning is much more than mindless group-work or research projects in the classroom. Indeed, such activity can be fundamentally aimless and disempowering, a form of work by which students are persuaded to involve themselves in learning what is of little or no value to them. Rather, active learning demands not so much the use of so-called student-centred methods, but rather the creation of a classroom climate and organization in which students become decision-makers along with their teachers.

This leads to a fifth component of critical pedagogy: its emphasis upon student empowerment leading to action for social change. Students must learn to think and to act. They must become both personally reflective and socially conscious. The central question is this: "... how do we make education meaningful by making it critical, and how do we make it critical so as to make it emancipatory?" (Giroux, 1981:3). Some of the answers have already been described: teachers must be theoretically informed; students' learning must be based on their culture and experience; at the same time, this learning must also include more traditional academic knowledge; classrooms must be centres of open inquiry that provide for and encourage meaningful student involvement; teaching methods must stress thought and action; the potential of human action ("the language of possibility") must be stressed; learning in the classroom must be directly linked to what is taking place outside the classroom; teachers and students must establish working relationships with groups working for social change outside the school; above all, teachers must see themselves as "transformative intellectuals (who) treat students as critical agents, question how knowledge is produced and distributed, utilize dialogue, and make knowledge meaningful, critical and ultimately emancipatory" (McLaren, 1989:23).

These five elements — here stated very broadly and no doubt over-simply — constitute the core of critical pedagogy.

They are pitched at a high level of generality, and it is to be regretted that critical pedagogy has not provided more description and analysis of specific classrooms in action. The best sources for descriptions of such activist classes can be found in the work of the Freinet movement in France or La maîtresse d'école in Québec (Freinet 1990, La maîtresse d'école 1989). Unfortunately, these sources seem to have had no impact on the English-speaking proponents of critical pedagogy. Peter McLaren, however, has provided two examples that are helpful in throwing light on what the English-speaking tradition of critical pedagogy can mean in practice. In reflecting on his teaching experience in Toronto, for example, he explains that, if he were to repeat it, he would involve his students in a programme of community study, including oral history, interviews, documenting local problems, investigating conditions and possible solutions and establishing links with social agencies, thus "... providing at least a beginning step in linking self-empowerment and social change" (McLaren, 1989:233).

McLaren also describes a technique for leading students to think more deeply about their attitudes to questions of sex and gender. He asks his students what they consider appealing and attractive in the opposite sex. Using this as a springboard for discussion, his class then looks at sexual stereotyping and gender bias as constructed through advertising, the media and so on, before going on to watch a video analyzing how Hollywood has portrayed women. The whole exercise concludes with students being asked to reconsider their attitudes to sex and gender and explain how they might have changed. In McLaren's words: "Students are thus encouraged to sort through the contradictions of their own experiences; they are given the chance to raise a fundamental question put forward by Giroux: What is it this society has made of me that I no longer want to be? In short, students are asked to look at their everyday taken-for-granted experiences (the ideologies of everyday life), as possible sources of learning" (McLaren, 1989:236-7).

Critical pedagogy has been much influenced by the work of Paolo Freire and, given the importance of Freire's contribution to pedagogical theory and practice, it will be useful to give his work special consideration. Certainly, anyone interested in the link between pedagogy, citizenship and social change cannot afford to ignore him.

Freire is a Brazilian educator whose contribution lies in both the theory and practice of pedagogy, and indeed, in the connection between them. His theory arose out of his work and influenced his further practice, so that for him theory and practice are and must necessarily be interconnected. Theory that has no impact on practice he condemns as verbalism. Practice that pays no attention to theory, he similarly condemns as mere activism. Rather, practice and theory must be mutually connected so that they contribute to each other. Freire calls this praxis, which he has described as "… the action and reflection of man (sic) upon his world in order to transform it" (Freire, 1970:66). For Freire, praxis is also a necessary part of being human. To be fully human, in his view, means to be the subject not the object of existence. One cannot be fully human when at the disposal of others. To be human means to be able to take control of one's own existence, to make decisions, to take action, to think and exercise one's power, not selfishly or ruthlessly but in the full awareness that one's actions affect and involve other people, who in turn have the right and the need to be truly human. This concept of praxis is central to Freire's theory of education and to his pedagogy. If teaching does not empower students to understand their world in order to transform it for the better, then it is not worth pursuing.

So seriously and successfully did Freire make this connection between practice and theory that the Brazilian military imprisoned and then deported him in 1964 as a threat to their regime. His particular task was to work with the poor and dispossessed in north-eastern Brazil in order to teach them literacy. But he quickly realized that literacy was not something that stood alone. It was part of a complex of other problems, of which it was not necessarily the most important. It was, so to speak, the tip of the iceberg resting on a base of poverty, powerlessness and lack of self-awareness. The poor were oppressed not only politically and economically, but also culturally. The dominant groups in society did not allow them to participate in the dominant culture while, at the same time, they were destroying the culture of the poor themselves. As a result, the poor came to see the world through the eyes of their oppressors, even identifying with them and blaming themselves or fate for their poverty and weakness. Thus, they became agents of their own oppression. Moreover, the only way they could see out of it was escape (as in drunkenness), or imitation (by themselves oppressing someone weaker than themselves), or by working for their oppressors, or, remotely, by replacing their oppressors and becoming oppressors themselves. In this last case, social institutions did not fundamentally change. The nature of power and of the way it was used remained the same except for the fact that there was a change in the holders of power — a situation which Freire sees as typical of many revolutions.

Schools are deeply implicated in all of this. They serve to transmit the dominant culture (i.e., the values and beliefs of the dominant group) and to decide who will receive it. At the same time, through their choice of subject matter and selection of curricula they deny the legitimacy of other cultures and values. An easily understood example of this process can be seen in the way in which for years Canadian schools sought to assimilate native children into Euro-Canadian culture (or a particular version of it), to the point of separating children from their families and communities and punishing them even for using native languages. Thus, for Freire, there can be no such thing as politically neutral education. Teachers are on the side either of the oppressed or, whether consciously or by default, the oppressors. They are never neutral. For those whose values are not reflected in the school curriculum, schools are a form of "cultural invasion." They serve to deny the validity of many students' experience and knowledge, which are thus treated as valueless. Instead of seeing themselves as knowledgeable and able to learn more, many students come to see themselves as ignorant and even stupid, and unable to learn at all.

So far as pedagogy is concerned, Freire puts the blame squarely on the transmission model that has dominated schools and which he calls the "banking" model in which teachers place deposits in the empty accounts that are students. Freire summarizes the main elements of banking pedagogy this way:

- teachers teach and students are taught;
- teachers know everything while students know nothing;
- teachers think and students are thought about;
- teachers talk and students listen;
- teachers control and students are controlled;
- teachers decide and students obey;
- teachers act and students can act only through the actions of their teachers;
- teachers select subject matter and students accept it;
- teachers substitute their personal power for the authority of knowledge and so deny the freedom of students;
- teachers are the subjects of the learning process; students are only objects (Freire, 1970:59).

In Freire's view, this pedagogy suffers from serious and irremediable defects. First, it treats students as totally passive beings, whose sole task is to accept all that their teachers tell them. Second, it constitutes a form of bad faith since many students, even those who do not resist their teacher, will know that what they are learning is mere ritual, devoid of real meaning. Third, it flies in the face of what we know about how people learn, which is by solving problems that arise from their own experience. Fourth, it disempowers students, making them mere receptacles, objects of someone else's experience, not subjects of their own. Fifth, it unduly narrows the choice of teaching techniques, to the point that teaching becomes predominantly narration, or teachers talking to students. "Education", wrote Freire, "is suffering from narration sickness" (Freire, 1970:57) and words, rather than acting to stimulate personal and social change, become "... a hollow, alienated and alienating verbosity" (*ibid.*). Finally, the banking model acts as a form of oppression. It prevents the growth of critical consciousness, of understanding and therefore acting on the world, by denying the importance, and even the reality, of students' own experience. Both deliberately and by default, it accepts the world as it is and refuses to consider the world as it could be. It removes students from the world in which they actually live. In Freire's words, it sees students *in* the world but rejects the possibility of their being *with* it, and thus acting upon it. Students count as nothing: "... verbalistic lessons, reading requirements, the methods of evaluating 'knowledge', the distance between the teacher and the taught, the criteria for promotion: everything in this ready-to-wear approach serves to obviate thinking" (Freire, 1970:63). Pedagogically, therefore, as well as politically, philosophically and psychologically, the banking model stands condemned.

In its place, Freire proposes a pedagogy consisting of two components: problem-posing and dialogue.

Problem-posing means exploring problems that students accept as real and therefore meaningful. Rather than beginning with a curriculum that is somehow "out there" and trying to interest students in it, teachers should use as their starting point problems and concerns that students identify or accept as important. This does not mean that students will necessarily be able easily to identify these problems. If they have become truly part of the culture of silence, they might fail to see the problems that exist, or at least to identify them to a teacher. Thus, although Freire emphasizes the importance of beginning with students' experience, of teaching *with* students rather than *to* them, he also reserves a particular place for the teacher. The teacher is not simply to abdicate his or her responsibility for seeing that students learn, but rather to add his or her knowledge, skills and experience in order to help students see their world in a new way. There is a risk in this of manipulation, that Freire does not altogether dispel, though it must be noted that he constantly emphasizes the crucial importance of students and teachers working together, so that "... the teacher-of-the-students and the students-of-the-teacher cease to exist and a new term emerges: teacher-student with student-teachers" (Freire, 1970:67).

This concept of teachers and students working together, with teachers working from students' experience and concerns but bringing to them their own insights and wider experience, introduces Freire's belief in dialogue as the central element in effective pedagogy. Freire makes it very clear that dialogue is much more than simply discussion. It is obviously not one person "depositing" knowledge or ideas in another, but nor is it a so-called exchange of ideas, in which, in fact, one person does all the producing and another the consuming, nor a physical argument or debate in which one wins while another loses. Dialogue is not competitive, but cooperative. It is not an interaction between one-who-knows and one-who-learns, but a process in which people collaborate as both knowers and learners, in which all contribute. It is an "act of creation", not of transmission or domination (Freire, 1970:77). For Freire, three qualities are necessary if it is to be successful: love, humility and faith. If teachers do not love the world and its people, they will not be able to enter into dialogue. They must respect students, treat them as fully human and be dedicated to their well-being. They must respect them for what they are and what they might become. Secondly, humility is necessary: teachers must give up their traditional power and authority; they must see themselves as learning from their students, as fellow-workers and comrades, not as superiors. Thirdly, faith is needed, for without faith in people's ability to grow, to remake themselves, to become more fully human, dialogue is pointless. Taken together, love, humility and faith make dialogue possible (Freire, 1970:79).

In other words, dialogue is quite different from simple discussion or conversation with students. This kind of informality can be manipulative as teachers seek to find a good relationship with students but do not otherwise change their views of what it means to be a teacher. To use the distinction made in Chapter 1, dialogue is not a technique but an approach. It demands a new way of thinking from teachers: "Dialogue is the sealing together of the teacher and the students in the joint act of knowing and re-knowing the object of study" (Shor & Freire, 1987:4).

At the same time, this does not mean that teachers must disown their skill or expertise and leave everything to their students. The teacher may, indeed, select what is to be learned but not in any sense that he or she knows everything that is to be known about it. As Ira Shor puts it: "The teacher selecting objects of study knows them *better* than the students as the course begins but the teacher *re-learns* the objects through studying them with the students" (Shor & Freire, 1987:14). Freire himself has emphasized this point: "... my position is not to deny the directive and necessary role of the educator. But, I am *not* the kind of educator who *owns* the objects I study with the students. I am extremely interested in the objects for study. They stimulate my curiosity and I bring this enthusiasm to the students. Then, both of us can illuminate the object together" (*ibid.*:15).

Dialogue cannot be separated from content, however. It is not a technique that can be more or less mechanically applied to any topic. It arises from topics in which students have an interest and to which they can make a contribution. In a pedagogy of dialogue, content should arise from the experience and concerns of the students, though these may not be immediately obvious to the teacher. It should consist of "... the organizing systematization and developing 're-presentation' to individuals of the things about which they want to know more" (Freire, 1970:82). One can see here another version of Freire's conviction that education can never be politically neutral. It always embodies some choice of values and views. It must inevitably support the *status quo* or work for social change. If it is to do the latter, and especially if it is to contribute to students' ability to improve their lives without exploiting others, then it must help them to see their world as it is in order to make it something better. As Freire puts it: "The starting point for organizing the program content of education or political action must be the present, existential, concrete situation, reflecting the aspirations of the people" (Freire, 1970:85). The teacher's task is to find out what students know, to help them reflect on it, to set it in a larger context, to help them make connections, to 're-present' their view of things, "... not as a lecture, but a problem" (Freire, 19970:191).

Freire describes this as "situated pedagogy" because the teaching is situated in the experience of students. He also recognizes that there are other ways of achieving the same goal. Choosing content from students' culture and experience is one option, but another is to study more "academic" topics in a situated manner, for example by "… inserting biology or history or nursing or economics into their social contexts" (Shor & Freire, 1987:19). Freire gives as an example a Brazilian physics professor who gets his students asking ordinary people how they understand the world and its working and uses this data, combined with students' own reflections, to approach the subject of physics. Freire concludes: "I am not against a curriculum or a program, but only against the authoritarian and elitist ways of organizing the studies. I am defending the critical participation of the students in *their* education" (Shor & Freire, 1987:21). As Ira Shor notes, this kind of teaching serves other purposes also, not least by "… challenging the students' learned passivity" (*ibid.*). For example, they take on new and unfamiliar responsibilities; they deal with non-university people; they see their own and others' thought as a research problem; they are freed from the prescription of their teacher and textbook.

It is tempting to say that students are thus "empowered," were it not for the fact that Freire has expressed his reservations about the word. He fears, especially in a North American context, that empowerment has become a purely individualistic notion: "… if you are not able to use your recent freedom to help others to be free by transforming the totality of society, then you are exercising only an individualist attitude towards empowerment or freedom" (Shor & Freire, 1987:23). This brings us back to Freire's insistence that education cannot be neutral and that it must be directed towards individual and social transformation, in the first case by giving people the intellectual and other skills to take control of their lives and, in the second, by building the kind of society that makes growth and development for everyone possible. As Freire puts it: "This makes empowerment much more than an individual or psychological event. It points to a political process by the dominated classes who seek their own freedom from domination, a long historical process where education is one front" (Shor & Freire, 1987:25). Whereas banking pedagogy assumes permanence and looks to the past for its standards of judgment and value, the pedagogy of dialogue emphasizes the process of becoming and assumes a "revolutionary futurity."

Feminist Pedagogy

The starting point of feminist educational theory is the determination to end the unequal treatment of boys and girls, and men and women, at all levels of the educational system, and to eliminate the educational sources of gender inequality. Girls, for example, are under-represented in such subjects as science and technology. Conversely, they are over-represented in others, such as home economics and the humanities. They were also, until recently, under-represented in university-entrance programmes in high schools. The standard view of education for girls was that they did not need much of an education, since their destiny was to become wives and mothers, leaving the "real" work to be done by men — a formulation which valued certain kinds of work (namely, paid work done by men) and devalued others, such as child-rearing and housework. Not only did most girls receive an education inferior to that of boys, but there were few role models for them to follow. In the schools, women were concentrated in elementary school-teaching and thus denied the relative status and prestige of their high school colleagues. Principals and school administrators were — and still are — mostly men. In the universities, the vast majority of professors were and are male, except for faculties such as nursing and human ecology.

Not surprisingly, therefore, the initial feminist interest in education was to redress this sexist bias. It quickly became obvious, however, that much more was involved than balance between the sexes. It has proved very difficult to correct gender imbalance, except in certain limited areas, indicating that the exclusion of girls and women from education is not simply a question of the biases of male educators, though these cannot be ignored, but of a systemic or structural fault. There is something embedded in the very structure of education that serves to penalize women. This realization directed attention to, among other things, the curriculum and the ways in which it was taught.

It is not a new discovery that the standard academic curriculum largely ignores women, but recent research has made the nature of the problem more obvious than ever before. Virtually every subject in the curriculum, at both school and university levels, has now been investigated and found either to ignore or undervalue women and women's experience, while at the same time treating men and men's experience not only as all that is important, but as representative of both sexes. In Dale Spender's words: "Most of the knowledge produced in our society has been provided by men.... They have created men's studies, for, by not acknowledging that they are presenting only the explanations of men, they have often 'passed off' this knowledge as human knowledge.... They have, in Mary Daly's terms, presented false knowledge by insisting that their partial view be accepted as the whole" (Spender, 1981:1-2). Thus, one of the first questions that feminist pedagogy teaches us to ask of any curriculum, book or teaching material is: where are the women and what is said about them?

Correcting the male bias of curricula and subject matter quickly proved to be much more than a question of simply filling the gaps, or inserting women into the silences of the curriculum. For one thing, to do this meant accepting the curriculum as it stood, not questioning its assumptions or priorities, and trying to find a place for women to be included. For another, it meant ignoring the increasingly obvious reality that to include women and women's experience, means rethinking and reshaping the values and premises on which the curriculum is based. As a U.S. commentator put it: "First you study women to fill in the gaps, but then it becomes more complicated because you see that the gaps were there for a reason" (McIntosh, 1983:10).

The gaps were in part a matter of semantics, with words being used to value male experience at the expense of female, or to treat male experience as universal, as in the case of such words as "man" or "mankind" or by the use of the masculine pronoun. To take an example, Dale Spender has noted the sexist biases implicit in the psychological terms "field dependence" and "field independence." These terms are used to describe the ability to identify a figure embedded in a "field", or visual context, with men showing more "independence", whereas women, who tend to give more attention to the context as a whole, are found to be more "dependent." In western culture, independence is generally seen as more desirable than dependence, and so the very terms themselves, far from being simply technical expressions, carry social connotations and implicit social values. Spender speculates on what connotations would follow if other terms had been invented, for example "context awareness" (female) and "context blindness" (male). Words can also be used to include some experiences and exclude others, as, for example, in the case of "work," which in historical and sociological research is still typically used to describe paid, publicly visible work of the kind historically done by men, though now increasingly by women, and to ignore the unpaid, less visible work done typically by women in the form of housework, family chores and childrearing.

Besides semantic problems such as these, curricula typically have ignored women's experience as a form of worthwhile knowledge. Great literature has been seen as typically written by men and about men. History has literally been his-story. The social sciences have largely ignored women as experimental subjects. The physical sciences have pretended that gender differences are irrelevant to their concerns. When women have appeared in the curriculum, for example in history, it is because they have "made it" in a man's world on men's terms. Such an approach is obviously unfair to women. It also ignores the reality that the man's world depends upon a vast amount of largely unseen female labour. As Dorothy Smith puts it: "Under the traditional gender regime, providing for a man's liberation... is a woman who keeps house for him, bears and cares for his children, washes his clothes, looks after him when he is sick, and generally provides for the logistics of his bodily existence" (Smith, 1990:18).

In such a traditional gender regime, it is also the case that men's and women's roles and experiences are generally dissimilar. Thus, to include women in a curriculum in any meaningful way will change the very shape of the curriculum. Viewed through women's eyes, for example, history often looks remarkably different from what it has been generally assumed to be. New topics of study emerge; new characters appear; accepted dates and "turning points" prove not to be so significant after all. As the U.S. historian, Joan Kelly, once observed of one accepted historical landmark: "... there was no renaissance for women — at least, not during the Renaissance" (Kelly, 1986:19). Here in Canada, a group of historians has raised the question of whether political or constitutional events, such as Confederation, are meaningful markers in the history of women. Instead, they identify three major turning points in the history of Canadian women: the transition from a pre-industrial to an industrial economy; the First World War; and the large-scale entry of women into the paid work-force (Prentice *et al.*, 1988:13).

Psychology, too, stands to be transformed by the attention now being given to women's experience. Carol Gilligan, for example, has taken issue with Lawrence Kohlberg's research on the development of moral reasoning. She has pointed out that Kohlberg's research involved exclusively male subjects, even though its results were generalized to both men and women. Putting it at its simplest, Kohlberg defined moral reasoning, and therefore moral behaviour, essentially in terms of rights and rules and duties, with the highest level consisting of commitment to universal ethical principles. But Gilligan has suggested that this is above all a male view, and that women see morality differently, defining it not in terms of rights and rules but of caring and concern, not of rights but of responsibility. In her words: "The moral imperative that emerges repeatedly in interviews with women is an injunction to care, a responsibility to discern and alleviate the 'real and recognizable' trouble of this world. For men, the moral imperative appears rather as an injunction to respect the rights of others and thus to protect from interference the rights to life and self-fulfilment" (Gilligan, 1982:100). Gilligan's work has not gone unchallenged but it is undeniable that it opens up the whole question of differences in male and female experience and of the way in which women see the world. It should be emphasized also that Gilligan is not arguing that one approach is in some way better than the other, but that both approaches are needed if we are to gain an accurate picture of human experience. It is not a question simply of redressing the balance in order to do justice to women. Rather, both men and women will benefit: "the conclusion of women's experience brings to developmental understanding a new perspective on relationships that changes the basic constructs of interpretation. The concept of identity expands to include the experience of interconnection. The moral domain is similarly enlarged by the inclusion of responsibility and care in relationships" (Gilligan, 1982:173).

Other feminist theorists have advanced similar arguments in other disciplines. Marilyn French has noted, for example, that men have conventionally thought of power as "power-over", with all the consequent assumptions about dominance, control and assertion, while women have thought of it as "power-to", involving not dominance but cooperation, not control but a commitment to a common activity to accomplish a particular task (French, 1985). Susan Moller Okin has argued that political philosophy must change. She concludes that: "There is no way in which we can include women, formerly minor characters, as major ones within the political drama without challenging basic and age-old assumptions about the family, its traditional sex roles, and its relation to the wider world of political society" (Okin, 1979:286). Jane Roland Martin has subjected educational philosophy to similar criticisms (Martin, 1985). History, literature, science and other subjects have all come under similar challenge.

Feminist scholarship, then, is fundamentally challenging the traditional view of the disciplines. It is also questioning the conventional academic assumptions of objectivity, of scientific detachment, of all the techniques and controls which are intended to remove the personal values and experiences of researchers from their research in order to produce something called science: impersonal, generalizable, detached, universal and objective. Particularly in the human and social sciences, feminists are arguing that the personal, the subjective, cannot be so easily removed from research and scholarly work — and indeed, should not be. They link the concern with "science," with objectivity and detachment, to male values and assumptions, which result in the dismissal of women's concerns for the personal and the interpersonal, for the human quality of experience. Thus, for example, feminists are generally sympathetic to qualitative research in the human and social sciences, with all its possibilities of uncovering the subjective, including the subjective values of the researcher, and are not committed to exclusively quantitative, and therefore allegedly more impersonal, methods.

From a feminist standpoint, it is simply not possible for researchers so completely to exclude themselves from their research. As Dorothy Smith puts it: "Taking the standpoint of women means recognizing that as inquirers we are thereby brought into determinate relations with those whose experience we intend to express. The concepts and frameworks, our methods of inquiry, of writing texts, and so forth, are integral aspects of that relation" (Smith, 1987:111). It is impossible to exclude the researcher's personal values, for even when we think we have excluded them, they will come creeping back in one form or another. In any case, the personal and the subjective, are too important and too valuable to be suppressed. Instead, they should be acknowledged and even celebrated. To quote Dorothy Smith again, speaking specifically of sociology: "An alternative sociology must preserve in it the presence, concerns, and experience of the sociologist as knower and discoverer" (Smith, 1990:23). Hoffnung has made a similar point about psychology in arguing against the inadequacy of a behaviourism which concerns itself only with assessing and analyzing external behaviour: "Feminist research requires not only the measurement of patterns of behaviour but also an understanding of why those patterns exist. It requires analysis of the situational context and the environment in addition to measuring the behaviour and cognition and feelings" (Hoffnung, 1984:10).

This feminist concern with the personal and the subjective, with reflection and experience, does not mean that objectivity disappears, only to be replaced by a subjectivity which will vary for all involved. The objective and the subjective must both be admitted into the world of research and scholarship. They must be used with and against each other so that their effects and insights work interactively. In this way, it is argued, we will benefit more than we would by relying only on one, especially if we deceive ourselves that objectivity is in fact attainable and is the only valid test of scientific respectability. In this context, subjectivity can be seen as imposing its own rigorous demands; it is not simply an unthinking celebration of personal feelings.

Mary Belenky and her colleagues have argued that the concern for experience and subjectivity, whether one's own or other people's, is also present in the way women acquire and reflect on knowledge. In this view, women's ways of knowing differ from men's, and do so in ways that have been devalued and condemned as second-rate by the dominant (i.e., male) tradition. Women, it is argued, do not easily accept the view of knowledge as dispassionate scientific truth, whose validity exists regardless of the knower. For women, knowledge is more personal; more contextual; more intuitive; more "connected" (to use Belenky's word) with context, with what one already knows and with what others know. Women see knowledge as constructed, with the knower being an integral part of what is known. In Belenky's words: "Women tend not to rely as readily or as exclusively on hypothetico-deductive inquiry, which posits an answer (the hypothesis) prior to the data collection, as they do on examining basic assumptions and the conditions in which a problem is cast" (Belenky *et al.*, 1986:13). Women, it is argued, are less likely than men to apply universal rules to a problem, regardless of context. They will think more subjectively, more concretely, more contextually. They will put human experience and need above rules and abstract principles.

It goes without saying that such qualities are not the results of biological endowment, but of socialization and upbringing. They are not related to the biological facts of sex but the social constructions of gender. They are not male and female, but masculine and feminine, and thus available to both sexes. Nor is it argued that either the masculine or the feminine is in some way superior, but that both are necessary if we are to benefit from all dimensions of human experience.

If this is to become possible, if both girls and boys are to receive a genuinely non-sexist education, then pedagogy becomes important and it is not surprising that a feminist pedagogy has now begun to emerge. It is not a seamless monolith, nor is it ever likely to be. Instead, it is a process of dialogue and discussion in which some common themes have emerged.

Feminist pedagogy first of all directs attention to the way in which women and women's experience are portrayed in the curriculum and its supporting materials — or, of course, not portrayed, as the case might be. In this regard, Peggy McIntosh has presented a useful five-phase classification of curricula. She used history as her primary example, but as she pointed out, the analysis can be applied to most subjects. Her five phases are as follows, though I have somewhat changed her titles (McIntosh, 1984):

Phase 1: The Absence of Women: In this phase, there is simply little or no mention of women in the curriculum, which thus serves to maintain the position of men and male experience as the criteria of status and worth.

Phase 2: The Inclusion of Women: In this phase, some women are included in the curriculum, but they are usually untypical, representing that handful of women who have learned to compete successfully in a male world on men's terms. Nothing changes in the curriculum by way of values or assumptions or even content, except that a few references are made to women.

Phase 3: Women as a Problem: In this phase, people begin to realize that the curriculum contains serious gaps and biases and, as a result, begin to examine the politics of the curriculum and to suggest alternatives.

Phase 4: Women as Subject Matter: In her example McIntosh calls this "women as history." It is a phase in which all women's lives and experience are incorporated into the curriculum, and as a result new topics are studied and old topics are studied in new ways. To use a McIntosh example, we ask not "Did women write anything good?" but "How did women tell their stories?" As a result, increasing use is made of non-traditional sources and materials and disciplinary boundaries begin to break down. As a further result of using new materials to ask new questions, the role of teachers changes. They become less of an authority, since they cannot readily draw on their knowledge, and more of an inquirer. The role of students also changes, since their experiences often become more relevant to what is being learned. In short, teachers become less powerful and students more powerful.

Phase 5: Subject-matter Redefined and Reconstructed: McIntosh said that she was not clear as to what this would involve, since it would represent a new way of thinking about knowledge, based on both men's and women's ways of experiencing, seeing and knowing the world, which has hardly yet come into being. In her words, it would be a "... circular, multi-cultural, inclusive curriculum which socializes people to be whole, balanced and undamaged, which includes rather than excluding most parts of life, and which fosters a pluralistic understanding and fulfils the dream of a common language" (p.33).

McIntosh's analysis confirms an argument already advanced: once one begins to integrate women's experience into the curriculum, the curriculum itself undergoes fundamental change. Feminist pedagogy is much more than an incremental process of filling gaps here and there. It also has far-reaching consequences for teaching methods and techniques, particularly concerning the role of teachers and students and the organization of the classroom.

Broadly speaking, feminist pedagogy aims to reduce the traditional power of teachers, to give more power to students, to give more emphasis to subjective experience and emotion, and to make classrooms more cooperative and democratic. Here is how two feminist theorists put it:

> ... for many scholarly researchers, the study of women involves a major methodological shift. They are moving away from the traditional search for objectivity and towards a multi-layered and comparative construction of social realities. In one's search, they acknowledge their own subjectivity, even as they try to transcend it by listening to, and drawing on, the experience of others. To go back to the classroom with this perspective is immediately to recognize its relevance to interactive

> pedagogies, which draw on students' experience not only for their own learning, but also to enrich the interpretations and materials of the discipline itself. (Culley & Portuges, 1985:36)

Jane Gaskell, Arlene McLaren and Myra Novogrodsky make a similar point: "Feminist pedagogy is based on a questioning of traditional authority relations between teacher and student and a distrust of bureaucracy. It eschews the separation of the public classroom from private experience, and does not recognize a clear distinction between emotion and reason. It is quite opposed, then, to traditional academic structures" (Gaskell, McLaren and Novogrodsky, 1989:197).

So far as teachers are concerned, feminist pedagogy aims to reduce a good deal of their power and authority, though there is no agreement on how far this reduction should be taken. Belenky and her colleagues speak of the "midwife teacher", arguing that the role of the teacher is not to put into students' heads something that was not there, but to help them deliver that which is there already. Belenky links this with Ruddick's notion of "maternal thinking", dedicated to the protection and nurturing of the vulnerable child. Thus, midwife teaching (1) protects and nurtures students' ideas, rather than subjecting them to destructive criticism or forcing them to conform to some norm; (2) fosters students' growth through providing help and support; (3) focuses on students' not teachers' knowledge; and (4) encourages students to use what they know in everyday life (Belenky et al., 1986:217-219). Schniedewind speaks of "shared leadership" with students, though it should be noted that the leadership is shared, not handed over. Schniedewind in fact retains a central role for the teacher. She says of herself that while she shares leadership, "... I don't have a totally egalitarian classroom. I take more leadership and have more power than any of the students" (Schniedewind, 1983:265). And, despite her acknowledgement that feminist values support replacing hierarchical authority with participatory decision-making, she observes that when a student makes unacceptable demands, for example of not wanting to write papers or to participate in group work, she refuses to cooperate: "... when any expectation is unacceptable to me, I suggest that the student insisting on it withdraw from the course" (p.264).

There is, in fact, no agreement in feminist pedagogy as to how directive teachers could or should be. There is universal agreement that mere authoritarianism is to be avoided and that teacher-student relations should be humane and democratic, though not necessarily egalitarian in the strict sense of the word. Most feminists accept that there is a place for the knowledge and experience of teachers, though only if they are used wisely and without manipulation. It can be that feminist pedagogy changes the power-structure of the classroom as a byproduct of its search for new subject matter and materials, though this will be more true of older students. For example, Culley describes a U.S. college-level class exploring women's historical experience through a wide variety of sources. She writes that since her students had to find these sources for themselves and since they opened up fields of knowledge unknown or new to the instructor, "... the nature of the course changed the authority structure in the classroom.... The role of the instructor was not to pass on a body of 'received' information or even to facilitate discussion of texts read in common" (Culley, 1982:88).

Whatever teachers make of their knowledge and expertise, feminists agree that they should establish relationships of openness, trust and cooperation with their students. As Belenky and her colleagues put it, teachers should strive for "connectedness," or the ability to empathize with students, to see the world as they see it, to work with them rather than over them. In Schniedewind's words, teachers must act upon the feminist values of "community, communication, equality and mutual nurturance," so that there is "an atmosphere of mutual respect, trust and community in the classroom" (p.262). In this same spirit, Martin speaks of the 3 C's of "care, concern and connection" (Martin, 1987:406-9).

Feminist teachers insist that these values should not only be acted on by teachers, but also that they should be fostered among students. Feminist pedagogy emphasizes interactive teaching techniques, with particular emphasis on dialogue, sharing and group-work. It values teaching techniques according to "the extent to which a community of learners is empowered to act responsibly toward one another and the subject matter..." (Shrewsbury, 1987:6). The phrase "community of learners" is interesting here, in that it changes the traditional concept of what it means to be a student: "... a classroom characterized as persons in a net of relationships with people who care about each other's learning as well as their own is very different from a classroom that is seen as comprised of teachers and students" (Shrewsbury, 1987:6).

Teachers are included as members of this community. Instead of acting as a combination of classroom managers and walking encyclopedias, responsible for shaping their students (a view nicely depicted in *The Prime of Miss Jean Brodie* and, in a different way, in *The Dead Poets' Society*), they should reveal themselves as learners along with their students. This is one beneficial side-effect of seeking out new topics and new sources, for it makes the students, not the teacher, the experts in their particular topic. Also, if teachers take up a research topic together with the class, it helps to demystify the teacher's role, to show students that their teacher is still learning and that learning is a process that never stops. Such a switch in roles can also have an impact upon the classroom: "If the teacher should take a research topic along with the class and participate with the students in the reporting of findings, a real change could take place in the classroom atmosphere" (Gilligan *et al.*, 1989:296).

This atmosphere will also be influenced by teachers' attention to personal subjective experience, both their own and that of their students. Feminist pedagogy follows feminist theory in its scepticism concerning objectivity and rule-governed knowledge. There are at least two aspects of this. One is a matter of attending carefully to students' concerns; the other involves the organization and conceptualization of knowledge.

Regarding students' concerns, feminist teachers take at least these steps: (1) they ensure that students are confident and relaxed enough to voice their concerns; (2) they respond to them and do not ignore or dismiss them when they are voiced; (3) they incorporate them into their teaching and connect them where appropriate into the curriculum; (4) they show students they are not alone and without help; and (5) they work with them constructively and non-judgmentally. Teachers should also be familiar enough with the appropriate research to understand and listen for gender differences in expressions of concern, both direct and indirect. Gilligan, for example, has argued that differences in moral reasoning can be seen by teachers as differences in intellectual powers, with resulting damage for girls: "... girls who appear to exemplify lower levels of cognitive functioning in early adolescence in fact may be resisting the detachment which characterizes abstract or formal reasoning" (Gilligan *et al.*, 1988:iii). Indeed, schools reward abstract learning more highly than they do connected or relational learning, thus favouring boys at the expense of girls, and so unduly limiting everyone's thinking. Above all, teachers must learn to act without pretence and to respond appropriately. Nora Lyons provides an example of a high school history class where the teacher was explaining the political arrangements made between southern Democrats and Republicans in a U.S. presidential election. The teacher was approaching the topic through an academic analysis of the functioning of political systems when a girl broke in and asked what reasons the politicians had to trust each other. The teacher decided that the girl was missing the point but Lyons analyzes it differently. In her view, the girl was working from a different premise: "... the logic she sought was not the logic of a system. Rather, she sought the logic of understanding..." (Gilligan *et al.*, 1989:69). Lyons goes on from this to make a more general point about pedagogy: "It is this approach to learning, with its different concerns and interests, that educators need to understand better and for which they must listen. They also need to make opportunities for this voice to be expressed and heard." Students' concerns, then, must be responded to, for they are the genuine expression of students' felt needs. They do not necessarily stem from personal crisis, but might emerge as part of the process of growth and development. In either case, they fall within the teacher's responsibility, especially in a feminist pedagogy of caring and connectedness.

This marks one manifestation of the personal and subjective; the other arises from the need to include the subjective element in our view of knowledge. Enough has been said about the feminist distrust of the view that equates scholarship and science with objectivity. From a feminist perspective, not only must the curriculum be taught in ways that allow for the exploration of the personal feelings of those under study, but it must also allow students to explore and refine their own feelings and reflect upon and extend their own experience. Personal opinions and judgments are to be encouraged. Such techniques as interviewing, the keeping of journals, dialogue and discussion, are to be stressed. Cognitive and affective learning are to be integrated. Belenky and her colleagues link this explicitly with their theory of women's psychological development, arguing that "... for women, confirmation and community are prerequisites rather than consequences of development" (Belenky *et al.*, 1986:194). Thus, feminist pedagogy welcomes topics and techniques that combine the intellect and the feelings: simulation, role-playing, drama, song and poetry, readings, journals, brain-storming, classroom celebrations, and so on.

Finally, feminist pedagogy sees a link between learning and action. Given feminists' desire to change society from its current male-dominated ways and beliefs, it is not surprising that they make a connection between pedagogy and social action. Worthwhile pedagogy, in their view, is that which, while respecting students' autonomy, empowers them to act more effectively in the world, both at the level of the personal and more broadly in the public sphere. This is the pedagogical application of the principle that the personal is in fact the political. In any event, feminist pedagogy is insistent that teachers must enable students to see the connection between what they are learning and their own lives and to act upon it. This might take the form of community development, or political action, of working on a school-community issue, of becoming involved at the local provincial, federal or even international level, but, whatever its form, action must result from education.

Obviously, feminist pedagogy shares many links and similarities with other movements in education. In Schniedewind's words, it means to teach "progressively, democratically and with feeling." It "implies that we enter into a dialogue with our students, meeting them as human beings, and learning with them in community" (Schniedewind, 1983:270). Its central values are community, cooperation, empowerment and social action. It is a pedagogy which sees a clear connection between the personal and political and which understands the political implications of pedagogical practice.

Chapter Three

TOWARDS A PEDAGOGY FOR DEMOCRATIC CITIZENSHIP

Teaching and Learning

The pedagogies described in the previous chapter have certain features in common that mark them off from transmission pedagogy, and that can be summarized as follows:

- Teachers no longer monopolize the front and centre of classroom action.
- Teachers become less instructors and more facilitators of learning; less actors and more stage managers, though never totally one or the other.
- The image of the student as an empty vessel or a blank slate is rejected.
- Students are seen as active participants in and shapers of their own learning.
- Classrooms must be open and democratic. characterized by sharing, trust and mutual respect among students and between teachers and students.

- Teacher-student relationships must become more equal. Teachers must see themselves not as wielders of power, whether on their own behalf or as agents of the wider society, employed to educate students for their own good, but as people whose job it is to help students grow and develop.
- The key goal is student empowerment. What is seen as important is not that students learn a lot of facts for their own sake, or do well in tests and exams, but that they become more independent, more in control of their own lives.
- Curricula are treated very flexibly and are certainly not seen as something that must be imposed on students for their own good, whether they like it or not. All these pedagogies reject any concept of the curriculum as something that stands apart from students, expecting them simply to learn what is put before them regardless of its relevance to their own lives.
- Finally, all these pedagogies adopt a problem-posing approach to learning and teaching. They see good lessons as those that raise problems for students, not in the sense of exercises to be completed or obstacles overcome, but of genuine questions of interest and concern, though they do not agree on whether these problems must necessarily arise from students' concerns or whether they can be legitimately designed by the teacher.

These common features should not be allowed to obscure the differences that also exist among the pedagogies. For example, just what should be the role of a curriculum? Just how directive should teachers be? How much authority and responsibility should be given to students? What is the appropriate balance between the academic/intellectual and the personal/social goals of education, and can they even be separated? These and other questions separate the pedagogies from each other, and indeed separate particular camps within each pedagogy.

Nonetheless, there is a common pedagogical ground on

which they all stand, that can in general terms be described as that which gives students a more central and active voice in their own learning, They see education not as something that is done to students, but as something that they do.

For our purpose, the most striking difference among the pedagogies is the extent to which they see themselves in political terms. While all of them contain some picture of what society should be like, only critical and feminist pedagogy take an explicitly political stand, combining a political-cultural analysis of existing practice and of existing society with a vision of a preferable social and political order. Inquiry/discovery pedagogy, on the other hand, is narrower in that it concentrates more on schools and less on their social context, and is more specifically individualistic, in that it concentrates on students' skills and values for their own sake.

Actually Existing Pedagogy

These pedagogies, however, remain the exception rather than the rule. They are more written about than used. Most classrooms still rely heavily on transmission pedagogy. We have not yet answered the question that Dewey asked as long ago as 1916: "Why is it, in spite of the fact that teaching by pouring in, learning by passive absorption, are universally condemned, that they are still so entrenched in practice? That education is not an affair of "telling" and being told, but an active and constructive process is a principle almost as generally violated in practice as conceded in theory" (Dewey, 1916:38)? All the research indicates that schools have not changed all that much since Dewey asked his question. Classrooms are still dominated by lectures, worksheets and question-and-answer routines. Moreover, this is largely accepted by students and adults as the way things are supposed to be. Schools, it seems, are the prisoners of their history and traditions. Since we know what schools were like in our own experience, we assume that this is how they must and should be.

At the same time, many students apparently realize that there is something wrong. The 1987 Radwanski Report in Ontario, for example, found that about 30% of students drop out of high school, and estimated that even of those who physically remain in school, some 20% or so have, so to speak, dropped out mentally. In Toronto, Bob Davis has reported that even these figures underestimate the problem, since dropping out of school is most common among working-class and minority children. He notes that, in Ontario, 62% of general level and 79% of basic level students do not complete high school. He quotes David Hickson, a Toronto social worker, reflecting back on his high school experience:

> Getting through high school was represented as just that, something to get through. The purpose of Grade 9 was to pass into Grade 10 and the final purpose was to get the diploma that the firms required.... Nothing was to be studied for its intrinsic merit or to make any kind of better world. You were merely moving from one classification to another to complete a diploma to qualify you for a job in a world which school made little comment on. (Davis, 1990:14)

Some Winnipeg high school students once told me the same thing when I asked them what they wanted to get out of Grade 10. Those were the words I used and they prompted an interesting but depressing response. That's exactly it, said the students, we want to get out of Grade 10. Why? So we can get into grade 11. And so on into Grade 12, and thus into (and out of) university. And these were "good" students (as their schools liked to call them) — middle-class for the most part, planning to go to university, placed in an "academic" program.

It is perhaps not surprising that in 1984 a Manitoba Teachers' Society survey reported that "student apathy and lack of motivation are perceived to be major concerns." This came out clearly in 1985 at a Winnipeg seminar on youth and the law, when students overwhelmingly complained that "their opinions are not taken seriously" and argued that: "they should have a greater part in making decisions that affect them" (*Winnipeg Free Press* 10 December, 1984/13 November, 1985). At the national level, Bibby and Posterski found a similar state of affairs, concluding that: "We have found that teenagers commonly perceive adults as insensitive to their problems. Teens further indicate that they are often not taken seriously. Some go so far as to say that an anti-adolescent mentality is fairly prevalent among adults. As a result, many feel alienated from adults and their institutions, including the family, the school, and the church" (Bibby & Posterski, 1985:xviii).

In schools, students are still often treated as empty vessels into which knowledge will be poured — or, even worse, as vessels that will not hold anything anyway, and thus should be treated gently but otherwise not disturbed. Bob Davis has described these two attitudes as "numbing and dumbing." In the first, students are numbed by an irrelevant curriculum and inadequate pedagogy. In the second, they are seen as dumb and thus unable to learn anything of any real importance. In both cases, enormous harm is done to people as a result of the heavy reliance on transmission pedagogy.

The impact of this is not equally felt by all students. There is a social class factor involved. Research has established quite conclusively that middle-class and working-class students do not receive the same education. In Canada, as elsewhere, wherever curricula are divided into academic, vocational, general and other tracks, working-class students are found overwhelmingly clustered in the so-called non-academic streams. Working-class students are far less likely to stay in school and to go on to college and university. Indeed, the conclusion is inescapable that schools serve to reinforce the influence of social class rather than to reduce it. Of course, a few working-class students always succeed and, by an effective semantic conjuring trick, this exceptional minority is held up to prove that the system is fair and equitable. After all, if they could do it, so could others. The fault, therefore, is located not in the system but in the students, or their parents, or their backgrounds. What has been called in other areas of society "blaming the victim," works in education too. Even more seriously, the victims come to believe it, blaming their "failure" not on the system, but on themselves.

This social class differential in education affects pedagogy also. It has been shown repeatedly that middle-class students get a better kind of teaching than do their working-class counterparts. They are given more autonomy; more interesting and intellectually challenging work; more scope for choice and independent decision-making; more opportunity for discussion and active learning. Conversely, working-class students receive a much lower level of instruction, with emphasis on low-level objectives; repetitive tasks; filling in the blanks; and so on. Schools see the difference not as between middle-class and working-class students, but as between "academic" and "non-academic" programmes (general, vocational, and the rest), and it is explained and justified on purely educational grounds, such as ability, aptitude, attitude, readiness for learning, and so on. These so-called educational arguments, however, simply camouflage a social reality. Even some conservative critics of the schools, such as Radwanski in Ontario, have come to reject any form of streaming or tracking on the grounds that it is not based on legitimate educational considerations, but rather reflects and reinforces the inequalities of social class divisions.

In fact, these divisions are based not only on social class. Race is also a factor. Black students, for example, are placed in dead-end, non-academic programs in numbers that far exceed the proportion of black Canadians in the population at large. Native students suffer the same fate, when they do not drop out of school altogether. And some immigrant children also do not get the full benefits of education. There are many factors at work here, including cultural differences, curricular biases and omissions, school organizational patterns, and teaching methods. There is some straight racism, but much of the problem is systemic rather than personal. There are, of course, students of all races who do well in school, but the fact remains that many non-white students suffer the same fate as students from working-class backgrounds. Indeed, race and class are often mutually reinforcing, since most minority students come from working-class backgrounds.

It is clear, then, that students do receive very different pedagogies. In the so-called less academic courses, taken predominantly by working-class and minority students, expectations and requirements are adjusted downwards to what teachers and administrators think is the appropriate level for the students. Indeed, the students themselves come to adopt this way of thinking, some because they genuinely believe it, others because it provides a convenient way of avoiding real work. "We can't do this; we're not the university entrance course," they say. Or, as some of my own students used to complain: "We're only general course students, you know."

Thus, expectations become a self-fulfilling prophecy. Labelled as non-academic, which everyone knows is a polite way of saying "slow," the students are taught accordingly. I once watched a young student-teacher teaching a class of so-called slow learners in Grade 10 geography. The topic was land-forms, and he gave the students ten minutes to read a short section in their textbooks on mountains. The students, of both sexes, looked about 18 years old, though they were still in Grade 10 (but then, they were "slow learners,") and their appearance suggested they were certainly street-wise. They were quiet and did their reading, but the student-teacher's first question met with zero response. "How many people," he asked, "do you think live on the tops of high mountains?" Receiving no response, he provided an answer and moved to other equally pointless and unproductive questions. When it was over, I asked why he had asked such questions of a group of street-wise young adults whose cumulative experience almost certainly outweighed his in complexity and depth. "You don't understand," the teacher told me, "these are 04 (the Manitoba jargon for non-academic) students. You have to keep everything simple." In England, such pedagogy has convinced David Hargreaves that for most working-class students, school is a prolonged exercise in humiliation. He writes: "My argument is that our present secondary school system, largely through the hidden curriculum, exerts on many pupils, particularly but by no means exclusively from the working class, a destruction of their dignity which is so massive and pervasive that few subsequently recover from it" (Hargreaves, 1982:61).

These are strong and disturbing words, but it is not certain that Hargreaves is altogether correct. Recently, Herb Kohl has made an extremely useful distinction between students who fail and students who refuse to learn what the school is trying to teach. The former sincerely try to do what the school wants but are not successful; the latter, in one way or another, reject the school. Both, however, are seen as failures, though their motivation is very different (Kohl, 1991). It seems to me not that students' dignity is destroyed, but that they preserve it by rejecting most of what the school has to offer and, in the tradition of clowns and jesters, undertaking a reversal of roles. Such, at least, is the message of another English study, Paul Willis's *Learning to Labour: How Working-Class Kids Get Working Class Jobs*. Here, in an English working-class school, the "lads" separated themselves from the "ear-'oles," or serious students, and set about turning school into a prolonged experience of "having a laff" (Willis, 1976).

In any event, whether such students come to accept the school's evaluation of them or simply reject it as irrelevant, they certainly put a barrier between themselves and the academic goals of their school. To that extent, at least, they confirm their label of non-academic.

In the process, teachers' and students' perceptions feed on each other. Rosenthal's and Jacobson's research on the "Pygmalion effect" suggests very strongly that, over time, how well or badly students do in school is more a reflection of their teachers' judgments of them than of any innate abilities (Rosenthal & Jacobson, 1968). In a similar vein, research has shown, in a study of kindergarten and early elementary school, how young students were sorted according to their teachers' judgments, which were much more a reflection of the children's social status, respectability, responsiveness, cleanliness, and so on, than of actual performance or estimated competence (Rist, 1973).

It should be emphasized that no-one is suggesting that teachers consciously apply a deliberate class or racial bias. Rather, they think in terms of what children are able to do, what they are ready for, and so on. Thus, for example, Rist's kindergarten teacher was not prejudiced against dirty children. The fact was that it was the clean children who coped better with school, who brought things for show and tell, who responded to the teacher's questions, who cooperated readily. It is hardly surprising, therefore, that they came to occupy more of the teacher's attention and came to do better in class. In Bourdieu's phrase, they brought to the school a "cultural capital," in the form of attitudes, knowledge and skills, that could quickly be turned to profitable use. In the teacher's eyes, they were simply better students, and each year they became better still. In education, as in the world generally, nothing succeeds like success. They demonstrated a principle to which we shall return: intelligence is not something that students have; it is something that they learn.

Teachers do not deliberately set out to maintain the inequalities that exist in society. They do not sit down and work out that society can only afford so many decision-makers, with everyone else being a decision-follower, and teach accordingly. Rather, their choice of pedagogy is an understandable response to the problems they face. Faced with a class of students who are not particularly interested in their school work, or at least not in the school work that the curriculum requires them to do, and who may not be especially fond of school at all, or who are weighed down by personal and family concerns, whose academic skills are below standard and who may not be inclined to cooperate or even to behave, it is understandable that teachers resort to one of three alternatives. Either they get tough and run their classes on military lines; or they turn to low-level, fill-in-the-blank exercises (sometimes both together in what Bob Davis calls the dittoes and discipline approach); or they give up any academic goals and turn instead to a kind of therapy, aiming to make their classrooms a happy social experience. It is, in any event, all very different from those classes of motivated students, where students at least do their work, know how to write an essay, and might even get enthusiastic about what they are doing.

In all this, teachers are almost as much the victims of the forces at work as are students — almost but not totally, since they do have some power to change things. So-called less academic students usually do not share their teachers' views of what is important, nor do they disguise their real feelings. Unlike their more academic counterparts, they are less willing to play the school game. They know that school is unlikely or unable to do much for them and thus see no point in taking it all that seriously. Nell Keddie suggests, in fact, that the difference between A-level and C-level students lies not so much in their understanding of what they study, but in their outward reactions to it and the teacher's judgments that result. Her conclusion is striking, for she argues that it might well be academic students' willingness to play the school game (one thinks also of Rist's kindergarten students) and to leave unchallenged the curriculum or their teachers, that leads to them being labelled as academic in the first place. In Keddie's words: "It would seem to be the failure of high-ability pupils to question what they are taught in schools that contributes in large measure to their educational achievement" (Keddie, 1971:156).

This discussion has been couched largely in terms of social class and its intersection with pedagogy, for class remains a fundamental component of schooling, though teachers often choose to ignore it. We are not yet a classless society, nor are we likely to be, nor in a capitalist economy can we be. However, class is not the only variable that influences pedagogy, and we must remember that what is said here about class can also be said about race, ethnicity and gender. The problems faced by native and black and by some immigrant students are well known. They are largely the victims of the same sort of labelling and restricted pedagogy as are working-class students. Indeed, in many cases, they are the same students anyway. Some brief comments about girls' education were offered in the previous chapter, and the whole topic is more fully dealt with in another book in this series, *Claiming An Education*. It is of crucial importance that teachers, when making pedagogical decisions, take the factors of class, race, gender and ethnicity into account.

As Dewey noted in 1916, we are thus faced with a contradiction. On the one hand, pedagogical theorists and reformers advocate active, participatory learning, with less emphasis on the teacher and more on the student; on the other, schools for the most part remain within the familiar tradition of transmission pedagogy.

Direct Instruction

Transmission pedagogy has in recent years received a new lease on life, owing to the research that has been done on teaching, or, more accurately, to the way in which the research has been interpreted and applied. Education researchers are now claiming that research on teaching has achieved a new level of both quantity and quality. Until at least the mid-1970's it was usual to complain that research on teaching either did not exist or was fundamentally flawed due to poor research methods. By the early 1980's, however, this complaint was no longer heard. In the third *Handbook of Research on Teaching*, published in 1986, researchers take obvious pride in what they have achieved. So far as pedagogy is specifically concerned, these research achievements have emphasized the importance of what has been called direct instruction, systematic teaching, effective teaching, or explicit instruction, though perhaps Good's term, "active teaching," is to be preferred.

The interest in direct instruction arises from the application of "process-product" research to teaching. This is research that seeks to identify which teaching processes have the most influence on the product of students' achievement, as measured on tests of students' knowledge or skills. In other words, and this is an important point to note, the research on direct instruction applies only to one particular form of students' learning, their performance on tests of knowledge and skills. The research findings are that the best performance is achieved under what might be loosely described as traditional teaching — in other words, transmission pedagogy. Students' performance on tests is highest, according to the research, when they spend maximum time on their learning tasks; when they are taught as a whole class, not in groups or as individuals; when teaching is expository and didactic, with clear explanations, demonstrations, repetitions and reviews; when they spend a lot of time doing supervised seat-work; when learning is sequenced into small, cumulative steps; when they follow classroom rules and procedures without question. To quote one research summary: "... students learn more in classrooms where teachers establish structures that limit pupil freedom of choice, physical movement, and disruption, and where there is relatively more teacher talk and teacher control of pupils' task behaviour." (Brophy & Good, 1986:336).

Rosenshine has synthesized the research on direct instruction and related work and proposed a model of what he describes as "effective instruction" (Rosenshine, 1986:377):

1. Daily Review And Checking Homework

Checking homework (routines for students to check each other's papers).

Reteaching when necessary.

Reviewing relevant past learning (may include questioning).

Review prerequisite skills (if applicable).

2. Presentation

Provide short statement of objectives.

Provide overview and structuring.

Proceed in small steps but at a rapid pace.

Intersperse questions within the demonstration to check for understanding.

Highlight main points.

Provide sufficient illustrations and concrete examples.

Provide demonstration models.

When necessary, give detailed and redundant instructions and examples.

3. Guided Practice

Initial student practice takes place with teacher guidance.

High frequency of questions and overt student practice (from teacher and/or materials).

Questions are directly relevant to the new content or skill.

Teacher checks for understanding (CFU) by evaluating student responses.

During CFU teacher gives additional explanation, process feedback or repeats explanation — where necessary.

All students have a chance to respond and receive feedback; teacher insures that all students participate.

Prompts are provided during guided practice (where appropriate).

Initial student practice is sufficient so that students can work independently.

Guided practice continues until students are firm.

Guided practice is continued (usually) until a success rate of 80% is achieved.

4. Correctives And Feedback

Quick, firm and correct responses can be followed by another question or a short acknowledgement of correctness (i.e., "that's right, Brian").

Hesitant correct answers might be followed by process feedback (i.e., "Yes, Linda, that's right because… ").

Student errors indicate a need for more practice.

Monitor students for systematic errors.

Try to obtain a substantive response to each question.

Corrections can include sustaining feedback (i.e. simplifying the question, giving clues), explaining or reviewing steps, giving process feedback, or reteaching the last steps.

Try to elicit an improved response when the first one is correct.

Guided practice and corrections continue until the teacher feels that the group can meet the objectives of the lesson.

Praise should be used in moderation, and specific praise is more effective than general praise.

5. Independent Practice (Seatwork)

Sufficient practice.

Practice is directly relevant to skills/content taught.

Practice to overlearning.

Practice until responses are firm, quick and automatic.

Ninety-five percent correct rate during independent practice.

Students alerted that seatwork will be checked.

Students held accountable for seatwork.

Actively supervise students, when possible.

6. Weekly and Monthly Reviews

Systematic review of previously learned material

Include review in homework

Frequent tests

Reteaching of material missed in tests.

It might well be that the research will not in fact support such a precise and prescriptive model as this, but it is nonetheless difficult simply to dismiss it. Some of it supports what common-sense would lead one to expect. It is not surprising, for example, that the more time students spend actively engaged on a task the better they do it, and it is worth noting that the research has discovered a surprisingly large amount of time being spent on non-academic activities (e.g., social chit-chat, organizing, disciplining) and large discrepancies among schools and classrooms in the amount of time spent on academic work, both in terms of time officially allocated to particular subjects and of time actually spent on them. Again, it is not surprising that, if teachers explain something clearly at an appropriate level for students to understand, then students do understand it better, though the research has discovered wide variations in teachers' ability to deliver such explanations. Sometimes, the research results do not confirm common-sense, however, or at least they contradict some widely accepted assumptions, for example on the value or effectiveness of group work and individualized instruction, or of discovery/inquiry techniques.

The research on direct instruction might appear to present some problems for the pedagogies outlined in the previous chapter. They emphasize student activity, discovery, group work and discussion, the democratization of teacher-student relationships, the flexibility of curricula, all of which contradict the traditions and assumptions of transmission pedagogy. But recent research seems to validate transmission pedagogy and show it to be effective. The question, therefore, arises: are the progressive pedagogies wrong, or is the research in error? Some researchers have dismissed the progressive pedagogies precisely because they are not research-based but derive from ideological and philosophical assumptions that have not been tested empirically. Such criticism ignores the obvious point that all pedagogies are the result of ideological and philosophical choices. It also misses the point that the success of progressive pedagogies, since they do not equate knowledge and citizenship with encyclopedic information and mechanical skills, cannot be tested by the same research methods as apply to direct instruction.

Beyond this, however, it is possible to reconcile the research on direct instruction with the progressive pedagogies. We need reject neither one nor the other, particularly if we keep in mind the nature of the research. There are four points to be made. First, the research has explicit limitations. Second, we should treat it cautiously. Third, it deals with only a part, not all of teaching. Fourth, it does not stand alone or unchallenged.

The limitations of the research are acknowledged by the researchers themselves. It has been done almost exclusively in American schools and what applies in the U.S.A. may not apply elsewhere, especially since education is so responsive to its cultural context. Moreover, it deals only with that part of teaching that concerns the teaching of specific knowledge and skills, and not with understanding and appreciation. To use the terms of Oakes and Lipton, it deals primarily with the "training" function of education and much less with "sense making." By the latter term, Oakes and Lipton mean "the mental process by which we construct individualized meanings and responses to our experiences. We figure out causes and effects, we apply knowledge gained from one experience to a different one, and we solve complex problems. Whenever we identify a problem, think about it and solve it, we make sense of our experiences" (Oakes & Lipton, 1990:30). The same contrast was made by Dewey in 1916 when he compared "automatic skill" with "personal perception" (Dewey, 1916:50). Both are obviously necessary, but it must be remembered that the direct transmission research deals primarily with the former, with the memorizing of factual information and the performance of specific skills. Its conclusions, therefore, should not be generalized into other areas of teaching and learning, such as the exploration and discussion of social issues, the analysis of value issues, the enhancement of creativity and personal response, and so on. Another limitation of the research is that most of it has been done in the elementary grades and so it might not apply with the same force at the secondary level, though some researchers say that the evidence does in fact apply to both.

Regardless of its limitations, we should, in any event, treat the research with some caution. The Rosenshine model of effective instruction, for example, is a composite drawn from a wide variety of individual studies, and thus does not apply in every detail to each and every classroom regardless of circumstances. Two of the leading researchers into direct instruction, Brophy and Good, make this point explicitly: "What appears to be just the right amount of demandingness (or structuring of content, or praise, etc.) for one class might be too much for a second class but not enough for a third class. Even within the same class, what constitutes effective instruction will vary according to subject-matter, group size, and the specific instructional objectives being pursued" (Brophy & Good, 1986:370). We must, then, be careful when thinking about the implications of direct instruction. It is not something that can be used automatically in any set of circumstances. To quote Brophy and Good once more: "... many findings must be qualified by reference to grade level, student characteristics, or teaching objectives" (Brophy & Good, 1986:360). While taking note of the research, teachers should resist any attempt to translate it into simplistic policy recommendations intended to apply to all classrooms. The research is helpful, but it is not a panacea. It might be that future work will also reveal it to be more limited than its champions allow. Schools have long been prone to band-wagons, where policy-makers leap on to some research and overgeneralize it, only to draw back when it proves not to be the magic solution after all. Teachers have seen it with continuous progress, open-area schools, integrated studies, and many other such innovations. The research on direct instruction should, therefore, be seen as tentative and suggestive, instead of conclusive, given our present state of knowledge.

Even if it were conclusive, it deals only with part of teaching and learning. The point has already been made that direct instruction applies only to the learning of specific knowledge and skills, and not to higher level understanding. This is not to dismiss it. Such learning is obviously an important element of education. To the extent that the research on direct instruction is helpful, it can be incorporated into any of the pedagogies outlined in the previous chapter. It becomes inconsistent with them only if direct instruction becomes the only and exclusive technique that teachers use.

Finally, it must be remembered that direct instruction does not stand unchallenged. Some years ago, for example, an English researcher, Neville Bennett, came to many of the same conclusions as those found in the direct instruction research. He divided teaching methods into three categories, formal, informal, and mixed, and found that on every count formal teaching (i.e., transmission pedagogy) was the most effective. At the time, opponents of alternative or innovative pedagogies hailed his research as proving what they upheld all along: traditional teaching is best. Teacher-centred pedagogy, tightly organized classrooms, well-defined curricula — these were the components of successful teaching. Many of the problems inherent in Bennett's research were ignored. For example, the categorization of teaching as formal, informal or mixed, was far from watertight. The judgments of students' performance were disputable in some cases. And, indeed, Bennett himself acknowledged that the research could not support the conclusions that were supposed to follow from it. But, even in the context of Bennett's research itself, regardless of its limitations, one finding went largely unnoticed: one of his most successful teachers was both formal and informal. Her teaching was formal in that she had a very clear sense of her curriculum and communicated it to her students, her expectations were clearly formulated and her content tightly organized. At the same time, her teaching was open to student participation; she encouraged a high degree of student activity; she adjusted her teaching to students' needs. In Bennett's words: "... the teacher was informal in attitude and behaviour... but almost half of the classroom activities were on some aspect of English and mathematics, the structuring of which was clear and sequenced" (Bennett, 1976:160). A moment's thought suggests that this finding is not particularly startling. Obviously, teachers need to be well-prepared; highly organized; have a clear sense of purpose and direction; and to give heavy emphasis to worthwhile academic learning, which is what Bennett would define as "formal." However, this need not and should not mean that they act as some kind of classroom bulldozer, sweeping all before them. It is not very startling to find that effective teaching consists precisely of a strong sense of purpose and organization combined with an ability to work with students cooperatively and openly.

That this might be so is suggested by another body of recent pedagogical research that stands in some contrast to direct instruction and that demonstrates the effectiveness and validity of cooperative learning, whereby heavy emphasis is given not to direct instruction by the teacher, but to students working together in groups with the teacher acting as organizer of learning rather than as instructor.

Cooperative Learning

The essence of cooperative learning techniques is the small group. Instead of being instructed as a whole class, students learn in small groups — deliberately mixed by ability, aptitude, ethnicity, gender and so on, since one of the goals of cooperative learning is to teach children to work cooperatively with others, regardless of their background. Together with this social goal, cooperative learning also aims to improve academic skills and students' self-concepts. It is an attractive and powerful combination and would appear to have important implications for those of us who wish to see pedagogy contribute to a different kind of citizenship and to the formation of a different kind of society.

At the same time, cooperative learning is not simply the application of group-work in the classroom. Group-work, like any other technique, can be good or bad. Students working in groups can waste time, learn undesirable messages, and simply reinforce their prejudices. Simply to put students into groups achieves nothing worthwhile of itself. Cooperative learning techniques employ group-work of considerable complexity and sophisticated structure. Moreover, cooperative learning insists that student-groups are far more than mere collections of individuals; they must be working towards a group goal, to which all team-members contribute, the attainment of which depends on the extent to which team-members work together. Robert Slavin, for example, argues that two conditions are essential for cooperative learning to take place. First, there must be a group goal; and second, there must be an individual accountability within the group. This is most often done by compiling team scores (on tests and so on) that are averages of individual scores, and recognizing team performance, for example in the form of certificates or of more concrete rewards (academic marks, free time, computer access, and so on.) There is, in other words a certain amount of competitiveness (among teams) in cooperative learning and there is a fairly heavy reliance on external stimulus and motivation. Both practices detract somewhat from the initial attractiveness of the approach and lead one to wonder whether students genuinely learn cooperative values from it, or whether they in fact go through the motions in order to win points. Cooperative learning seems designed not so much to produce genuine cooperation, as to teach students how to compete more successfully. However, although such reservations cannot be put aside, cooperative learning as a general pedagogical approach has a potential that should not be ignored. Instead of discussing this potential in general terms, it will be more useful to provide some specific examples of the various techniques available. The two that follow are the Team Assisted Individualization–Mathematics model of Robert Slavin and his colleagues, and the Jigsaw approach of Eliot Aronson.

Team Assisted Individualization-Mathematics (TAI) is intended for Grades 3-6, though it has been used with older students, and combines direct instruction by the teacher, cooperative group learning and individualized instruction. Its main elements are as follows (Slavin *et al.*, 1989-90:22-29):

1. Students are divided into heterogeneous groups of 4-5, that are changed every eight weeks.

2. Students work on carefully designed self-study mathematics units, according to their particular skill level.

3. Carefully organized procedures direct students' progress,

so that they can move through the units only as they successfully complete a certain percentage of tasks and problems.

4. When they need help, students turn first to their teammates and then to the teacher if necessary.

5. A student's readiness to write a unit test is determined by the student's work on the unit as certified by a team-member. The mark obtained on the test becomes part of the team average.

6. In every class, the teacher teaches specific mathematics content to small groups of students from different groups who are working at the same level.

7. Every three weeks, the teacher teaches specific content to the whole class.

8. At the end of each week, the teacher calculates team scores that are an average of individual scores on unit tests and of the number of units completed by each team.

9. On the basis of these scores, teams are designated as "super-teams," "great teams" or "good teams," with the first two being rewarded with special certificates.

A similar degree of complexity and organization, though in a somewhat different form, can be seen in Aronson's "Jigsaw" model (Aronson *et al.*, Beverley Hills, 1978). Here, students are assigned to heterogeneous groups of about five students each. Each student in each group is given materials dealing with a particular part of the topic under study, so that, for example, all the Number 1's in each group study the same thing, all the Number 2's, and so on. Their task is to become experts on their particular part of the topic in order that they will be able to teach the rest of the group. Each will have, so to speak, a part of the puzzle, but only when they work together will the pieces form the complete jigsaw. After they have had time for individual reading and study, the students will leave their groups and join "expert groups," one consisting of all the

Number 1's, the next of all the Number 2's, and so on. Each student in these expert groups will compare notes, discuss, quiz each other and ensure that their knowledge is as complete as possible. This done, they then return to their original groups to teach the other group members what they know. Once all the students have done this, with ample use of quizzes, study guides, outlines and so on, the groups should be able to demonstrate their knowledge, either on a test or in the form of a report or in some other fashion. It is possible also to incorporate in the evaluation scheme, a system of "improvement points" to reward not so much absolute performance as improvement over previous performance, and so provide some incentive for both individuals and teams to improve. Whatever is done, performance should be adequately recognized and should combine individual and group achievement.

Both examples — and many other techniques exist — show clearly that cooperative learning demands a high degree of organization, both in the form of the materials provided and in the teaching techniques employed. Above all, students need to be carefully prepared. The Johnsons have suggested that the following conditions need to be observed if cooperative learning is to work properly (Johnson & Johnson, 1989/90:29-33):

1. The need for the kinds of social skills demanded has to be understood and accepted by students.

2. Students must understand what kinds of external behaviour (speech, gesture and so on) demonstrate that the skills are being used.

3. Students must role-play the skills until they are familiar with them.

4. Students must analyze and evaluate how often and how successfully the skills were used in actual group work.

5. Student groups must be evaluated and rewarded in terms of how well they use the skills.

The basic point is clear: successful group work depends upon the use of social skills, including communication, trust, acceptance and support, and the ability to resolve conflict. These skills must be identified and taught: they must be used by students until they become automatic.

Of particular interest is cooperative learning's insistence on the importance of using heterogeneous groups, if genuine cooperation is to take place. This flies in the face of what schools often do, and of what parents and teachers often accept without question — that it is most sensible to organize students by ability, to the point of streaming or tracking them into different programmes — academic, vocational and the rest. On the surface, ability grouping has a certain common-sense appeal. It allows students to work at an appropriate level of difficulty. It prevents advanced students from being held back by slower ones, while also ensuring that the slower ones are not humiliated by falling behind. It makes teaching easier and more effective by allowing teachers to aim their teaching at the most appropriate level and not to dilute it by trying to cover a wide range of ability levels.

Behind these psychological arguments, however, lies a social reality. Ability grouping serves a system in which a minority of students is being trained to become leaders and the majority to become followers. Ability grouping, in other words, is an integral part of a society divided by inequalities of power and influence. Moreover, no-one ever has satisfactorily explained why it coincides so neatly with gender, class and ethnicity. It is difficult to accept that academic ability is apparently mostly to be found in middle-class students but much less in working-class, black, native and many immigrant students. In fact, recent research has shown that the selection of students into various ability levels often has little to do with ability at all, but instead with matters of attitude, background and expectations. Instead of adjusting programs to students, ability grouping in fact leads to the prejudging of students. In the words of the most recent researcher into this topic, Jeannie Oakes: "The result is that some children do not have access to classes in which academically and socially valued subjects are taught. Nearly all children can learn from good literature. Nearly all can learn a second language. Nearly all can benefit from studying algebra. Some will learn more, some less. Tracking excludes many children from ever being in some classes. Furthermore, when schools err in their judgment, they are more likely to underestimate than to overestimate what children can accomplish" (Oakes & Lipton, 1990:159).

The most damning judgment against ability grouping is that it condemns those students placed in the slower groups to an inferior education. Teachers expect less of them. They expect less of themselves. Over the years, perception becomes reality and the students lose interest in school, either dropping out, becoming disruptive or resigning themselves to cynicism and apathy. Regarded as slow, they come to act as though they are slow. They reserve their intelligence and curiosity for non-school activities. Well-meaning teachers deliberately adjust their teaching downwards to meet the supposed needs of these students for work that is concrete, here-and-now and relevant. Oakes describes the process well: "... their learning tasks most often include memorizing or copying answers and taking quizzes. Critical thinking and problem-solving, if they are emphasized at all, are presented in packaged programs; they do not emerge from a course full of valued knowledge. Low-ability classes are far from being 'relevant' and practical, as they are often claimed to be. Because teachers usually teach basic topics and skills out of context, learning tasks are often more abstract and removed from the real world than in high-ability classes. Since low-ability classes omit so much important knowledge, students who spend even a brief time in such classes can miss the experiences they need to reenter and succeed in higher classes" (Oakes & Lipton, 1990:161).

Despite this immense cost to the students involved and to society in general, the high-ability students do not receive that much better quality of education. Oakes and other researchers have demonstrated that so-called high ability students usually do no better when specially singled out than they do in mixed classes. Even when they do, the difference is marginal, and certainly not worth the cost that has to be paid by the students who are placed in lower classes. This is not education for democracy, or for any kind of citizenship worthy of the name. It is, instead, education for inequality. It makes eminent sense in the context of society as it exists, with its built-in inequalities of wealth, power and influence, both economic and political. It is totally unacceptable in any view of education as a force for social justice and democracy.

Thus, cooperative learning, with its emphasis on mixing students and teaching them to work together, and on making them more responsible for their learning, is a welcome pedagogical innovation. We must be careful of its more enthusiastic promoters, who seem to see it as a solution for all problems and who are inclined to describe any group activity, no matter how unorganized, as cooperative learning. We must certainly separate out those approaches that genuinely embody cooperative education principles, from those that merely claim to do so, for it is already on the way to becoming something of a fad. We need to question, also, its apparent reliance on external reward and stimulus, for we want students to cooperate not in order to win some prize, or to do better than their competitors, but simply because it represents a higher, more rewarding and more responsible way of living. If we believe in the cooperative community, the classroom is a good place to start.

Some of the clearest examples of the effectiveness of cooperative learning can be found in the work of Célestin Freinet, whose writings have only recently begun to appear in English (Freinet 1990a, Freinet 1990b). They describe various ways in which cooperative learning techniques can be incorporated into a broader scheme of pedagogy, school organization, and inter-school networks. Within this framework, Freinet actively promotes a socially conscious and activist curriculum. Those interested in finding alternatives to the reward schemes embedded in American cooperative learning projects will find them in some of the work published by the Québec collective, La maîtresse d'école (Maîtresse d'école, 1989: 29-31, 56-58).

The Role of the Teacher

In their different ways both direct instruction and cooperative learning point to one useful conclusion: if student learning is to take place, the teacher must play an active role in the classroom. To be opposed to transmission pedagogy does *not* mean to remove the teacher from teaching. It means a different role for the teacher but one that is no less important. To say this ought to be stating the obvious, were it not for the fact that there are teachers who feel that they should not "impose" on students. Their model comes from A.S. Neill's *Summerhill*, or from a misunderstanding of the British primary schools of the 1960's, or from Freire (or more accurately, a misreading of Freire). In their view, students must be decision-makers in education: only students should decide what they want to learn and when and how. The teacher's job is to stand aside until students are ready to learn. In the early 1970's this approach was supported from another direction also, as Ivan Illich, Everett Reimer and others argued for the "de-schooling" of society. In their view, schools could never escape their role as instruments of domination; they did not open students' minds but closed them; they did not foster development, they blocked it. Schools were too far gone to be reformed. The only solution was to abandon them and establish something totally different. By the late 1960's it had become customary to portray schools as hopeless and oppressive, serving to block and frustrate true development. Silberman called them "mindless"; Goodman wrote of "compulsory miseducation"; Reimer argued that school was dead; Illich promoted de-schooling; Kozol wrote of "death at an early age"; Friedenburg saw schools as fundamentally hostile to the young; the left generally saw them as instrument of the ruling class.

These, then, were bleak times for many progressive teachers. Convinced that the criticisms of the schools were largely accurate, we found them more difficult to ignore or rebut because they themselves came from our political friends on the left. Many of us began to question what we were doing. Were we, in fact, fooling ourselves in thinking that we were helping our students? Even worse, were we really supporting oppressive schooling by being part of the process at all? Was school reform absolutely impossible? Were we ourselves helpless victims of the system?

These were difficult and troubling questions, that struck at the very heart of our personal and professional lives. We had gone into teaching because we thought we could make a difference, not only for our students, but in the name of social change. Now we were being told that we were wasting our time or, even worse, that we were actually supporting the very institutions that prevented change. It was hardly surprising that some left teaching altogether. Others remained committed to teaching but abandoned the public school system and turned instead to free schools or alternative schools, that enjoyed a brief boom in the early 1970's. Many who remained in the public schools rethought their pedagogy. We became even more student-centred, we experimented with curricula, we were dominated by the search for relevance. We became extremely sensitive to anything that we thought might be seen as imposing on students. This was made easier by the elimination of province–wide external examinations and the general relaxing of school rules and regulations that took place in the 1970's.

As a result, many of us drew a wrong and dangerous conclusion. We came to think any form of directive teaching was wrong. So, on what might be called the educational left, progressive pedagogy was defined as one in which teachers played a subordinate role to students. These were the kinds of statements that became influential:

> In an informal classroom... the teacher is the facilitator rather than the source of learning, the source being the child himself (*sic*). Learning is something the child makes happen to and for himself, albeit with the teacher's aid, and sometimes at her instigation. (Silberman, 1970:268)

> The teachers begin with the assumption that the children want to learn and will learn in their fashion; learning is rooted in firsthand experience so that teaching becomes the encouragement and enhancement of each child's own thirst toward mastery and understanding. (Nyquist & Hawes, 1972:10)

> The underlying assumption of "informal" schools... is that in an enriched and carefully planned environment that supports the natural drive toward learning, children are able to learn mostly by themselves, from each other and from books. They learn in encounters with the things and people around them, and they do so at their own irregular and individual pace. They

> learn most intensely when they are interested and see the pertinence of what they are doing. The role of the teacher is important but quite untraditional: There are few, if any, whole-class lessons, no standardized tests, no meticulously detailed and rigidly enforced curriculum. (Scheir & Scheir, 1971:30-31)

The mistake we made was two-fold. First, we too easily accepted the view of schools as totally repressive. Only later, thanks to the more nuanced work of Apple, Giroux and others, did we see that schools were, in fact, arenas of conflict (to use Brian Simon's phrase) in which genuinely educational work was possible. Second, in rejecting what schools had traditionally done, we failed to consider that some things might be worth keeping. In particular, in rejecting transmission pedagogy, we assumed that it must always and inevitably be damaging to students.

The reality is, however, that there are times when straightforward teacher-talk is an appropriate form of teaching. A good lecture, delivering a well-told story or raising provocative questions or presenting an outline or a review of material that will be or has been covered, is easily justifiable. The essential point is that teachers will often have something worthwhile and interesting to say on a topic. If they do not, it is difficult to see why they are teachers. Presumably they will be more widely read and better-informed than their students (though not on all topics with all students — one of the most rewarding moments comes when a student knows more than the teacher and both realize it); and they have a clear duty to use their knowledge to lead students to things they would not otherwise have known. Lecturing, after all, can be thought of as a form of story-telling and as such, as long as it is done appropriately and well, has a place in the teacher's repertoire. As, indeed, do other aspects of transmission pedagogy. Even something as routine as giving notes or using a worksheet can be justified in certain circumstances. It is when transmission pedagogy is used as an approach instead of as a source of techniques to be used for limited purposes, that it becomes unacceptable.

Freire himself acknowledges that teachers play a directive role even in his dialogical approach to teaching. Dewey similarly recognized the teacher's responsibility to be pedagogically active: "The greater maturity of experience which should belong to the adult as educator puts him (*sic*) in a position to evaluate each experience of the young in a way in which the one having the less mature experience cannot do" (Dewey, 1938:38). He went on to note: "... guidance given by the teacher to the exercise of the pupils' intelligence is an aid to freedom, not a restriction upon it" (p.71).Similarly, both Freinet in France and La maîtresse d'école in Québec reject undirected learning (Freinet, 1990a: 54,56; Maîtresse d'école, 1989: 108-9).

This does not mean that teachers can ride rough-shod over their students. Good lecturers, for example, always make sure that what they have to say makes some point of connection with their listeners and provokes them to further thought. It is possible to make too much of the empty vessel analogy, since students are obviously to some extent empty of knowledge and experience and do need a certain amount of filling. The point is that when we give students knowledge (without drowning them in it) we should do so appropriately.

Teaching and learning, in other words, should be an exercise in cooperation, not in control. As Freire noted, teachers should not deny their superior knowledge, but nor should they exalt it into a mystique. They should use it to open students' minds, not to close them. They should teach in ways that are *authoritative* but not *authoritarian*. Authoritativeness comes from expertise and experience. Authoritarianism relies upon raw power and control. It is possible for one to slip over into the other, so that expertise is used as power, but it is neither inevitable nor necessary that this happens. Teachers can have authority based upon knowledge, reading, enthusiasm and so on, but can still invite and welcome challenge, criticism and argument. To be an authority in this sense does not mean laying claim to infallibility or refusing to admit ignorance. Indeed, the more secure one is with a body of knowledge and the more that this is recognized by others, the easier it is to admit not knowing. It is people (including teachers) who do not know very much who see every question or challenge as a threat to their credibility. It does students no harm to meet teachers who are in love with their subjects. One of the most fundamental goals of education is to convey a love of learning and enthusiastic, authoritative teachers are the best way to do so. Herb Kohl describes this when writing of his attempts to teach an uncooperative 14-year-old boy to read. At one meeting, the boy exploded and knocked Kohl's papers off his desk and Kohl exploded in his turn: "... next to the people I love, my manuscripts are the most important things in my life, and I told him so. I ranted on about how important writing and books were to me." Kohl observes: "I doubt that he had ever experienced an adult express so much care for learning and books — not for some relationship to a reading test or grade, but for books themselves" (Kohl, 1984:65).

There are, of course, many ways for teachers to demonstrate their authoritativeness, both formally and informally, through explicit teaching and example and more indirectly through their own behaviour. Here for example is one such teacher, as described by Edward Blishen:

> He used to give us free use of his private library at home. He used to bring us books in a perfectly natural way. He talked about books with joy and pleasure, and also when it was necessary — and it turned out to be often necessary — talked abusively about books. He had a habit as he passed between the rows of boys, of tossing a book into your lap as he went by with some murmur of: 'Sh — you'll love this,' or 'Sh — you'll hate this,' or best of all, 'Don't let anybody see that! Keep it quiet!' ... But what a sense of conspiracy he knew how to generate! Pedagogically he was an immensely ingenious man, though in fact in pedagogy he might have rated very low indeed. How simple was all that he did, and how good it was to be made part of his life as a reader! How influential to have this utterly natural exhibition by a grown-up, with whom you were constantly in contact, of the quality of a true reader who displayed before us, quite naturally, all the responses to books, rage as well as deep appreciation. How simple! (Benton & Fox, 1985:101)

This example nicely shows how a teacher's enthusiasm and authority need not suppress students, but, on the contrary, can stimulate their interest. It is not a case of the teacher hogging the spotlight and thereby turning the classroom into a solo performance, with the students being no more than spectators. If a teacher's activity does not stimulate or provoke student activity, then the teacher must carefully examine why this is so. The rule can be simply stated: the activity of the teacher must be such as to provoke activity by the students. There are obviously many ways to do this: using subject matter to raise questions of wider interest; linking it to students' concerns; asking open-ended questions; promoting the use of dialogue and discussion, both formal and informal; using cooperative learning techniques; giving students a voice in determining how they will approach a topic; making use of speakers, field-trips, simulation, role-playing and other ways of bringing a subject to life.

All too often, however, the operating assumption in many classrooms seems to be that children are ignorant. This, it is assumed, is why they are forced to attend school: to become informed — which usually means learning what their teachers already know. Certainly, acquiring knowledge is an important part of education. No-one can properly be called educated if he or she knows nothing. At the same time, it is important to remember that knowledge is precisely a part of education, not the whole of it. Teaching can be said to consist of information-giving and problem-posing, but too often the first excludes the second.

Thus, the crucial task is too easily seen as giving children useful knowledge. At best, what they do know — be it about license-plates, strategy or fantasy games, animals, music, sports or whatever — is seen as inferior knowledge. After all, if it were not inferior, it would be on the curriculum. If it is not there, then by definition in school terms it is not worth knowing.

This is misguided on two counts. First, it automatically downgrades students. Their ideas and experience are seen as of little importance. Think, for instance, of the implication of that all too frequent teacher response to a student answer: "No, that's not really what I'm thinking of." What the student wants to say is not all that important; it is what the teacher thinks that matters. This is poor teaching by any standard. The whole point is that students should learn to dissect an issue, to look at a range of viewpoints, to speak their mind; not to sit like the R.C.A. Victor dog, waiting for "His Master's Voice."

Second, it ignores the obvious fact that, thanks to the mass media and the increasing mobility of families, students in fact know a surprising amount. James Coleman has distinguished between an information-poor and an information-rich society, pointing out that school emerged in the former and served to provide the young with a window on the world. In an information-poor society, the school is a major source of information. A hundred years ago (or less), for example, it was largely in school that youngsters found out about the wider world they lived in. Schools served an expository, information-dispensing function. Today, however, we live in an information-rich society, with the young getting vast amounts of information from non-school sources. Despite this shift, the school continues to function above all as a dispenser of information. To some extent, of course, it must do so, but not to the exclusion of its problem-posing role.

Five examples might make these points more specifically. The first comes from Winnipeg and is taken from a Grade 9 history lesson dealing with the Industrial Revolution. The teacher wanted to avoid turning the topic into a list of inventors and inventions, of dead causes and results, or even of a graphic account of the abuses of child labour and other such evils. Instead, he was looking for a way to use the material to raise more substantial issues that would throw some light on contemporary society, connect it with the past, and stimulate the students to offer their own ideas and suggestions. The particular theme he chose was the impact of technology upon the way the Industrial Revolution turned us into a clock-oriented people who more and more organize life, not by natural rhythms, but by measured time. The concept of time is, of course, fairly abstract, and what the teacher wanted to do was somewhat sophisticated for this particular class. The problem was, therefore, how to deal with the topic without simply handing out dead chunks of information. The teacher began with the clock on the classroom wall and asked the students how on that day clocks and clock-time had affected their lives. They quickly responded with examples of alarm-clocks, clock radios, T.V. and radio schedules, school bells and so on, all drawn from their own experience. With this basis established, they were then asked what would happen to modern society if clock-time were somehow abolished, and they quickly saw that it would collapse. As a side issue, they embarked on some consideration of whether the clock was in fact the most important factor in modern life. In the course of the discussion, one student said that, without clocks, "we wouldn't know if we were late for school." The teacher picked up on this and asked how schools might change without clocks and, after several false starts, one student came up with the idea that they could pick up work at school, do it at home, bring it back for checking, and so on. This opened up the whole topic of the role of schools in modern society and of the organization of work, which brought everything nicely back to the Industrial Revolution. Throughout the lesson, history had been linked to the present; students had been encouraged to think, speculate and discuss; they had learned and thought about new information and taken-for-granted concepts, and in the process, though the teacher played an active role, they had in many ways taken charge of the lesson.

A second example comes from Newfoundland where Don Sawyer, as a new teacher, faced the problem of teaching English to a bored class with little previous experience of success. The students had until then been taught English in traditional ways, with a heavy emphasis on assigned readings, questions and attempts at "discussion." In Sawyer's words:

> It was a process that had dominated English for most of these kids and had turned many of them away from reading. What it had really taught them was that they could not be successful in any case. And they were also convinced that English could be no other way. The idea of English as having something to do with communication — alive, verbal and stemming from their own experience — was as alien as nuclear physics. (Sawyer, 1979:52-3)

To remedy this state of affairs, Sawyer abandoned the prescribed texts and turned instead to comic books, beginning by simply inviting students to read and talk about them. Upon this foundation, he asked them to invent their own super-heroes and super-villains and to put them in a story, a task that unleashed hitherto unused talent and energy: "The results were the first evidence of the brilliance and imaginativeness of which these kids were capable" (Sawyer, 1979:54). This was the initial step in a process by which Sawyer's students first gained some confidence in their own powers (an extremely important step, after years of being branded as failures) and, second, became more proficient in reading and writing generally.

The third example comes not from Canada but from Britain. The teacher, Phil Cohen, was working with a group of early-school-leavers in a special program designed to make them attractive to employers in an area of high unemployment. Traditionally this kind of programme sought to give young teenagers the personal and social skills, together with the basic information about jobs and how to find them, deemed necessary to get and perhaps even to pass a job interview. Cohen, however, went about it differently, beginning with an assortment of hobby magazines and career literature in order to get the students to compare their personal skills and interests with the requirements of the real world, while at the same time, making them aware of issues of power, control and definition, in the sense of thinking about who was establishing the agendas of thought and action. This was followed by a series of visits to different workplaces selected to illustrate issues of sexism in the workplace, unionism, management rights, and so on. These visits were reported through photo-essays, interviews and other techniques, "enabling students to interpret the emerging issues in the light of their own concerns." Initially, the visits were conducted with pre-scripted questions, set itineraries and all the apparatus of teacher-control, but the students quickly took on "collective responsibility for generating material which reflected their, not our, concerns" and told their teachers to let them get on with the job. Cohen tells of one instance when the students met a gang of telephone engineers working in the street. The conversation began awkwardly, until a girl asked one of the men if the job had any special perks. "Talking to young girls in the street, was the answer, and its naturalness released a flow of stories from the men about moonlighting and other fiddles, the skives they used to get up to when they were apprentices, and the importance of not having the gaffer on your back." It is worth quoting Cohen's assessment of this experience:

> ... a real rapport was established around the commonalities of a class experience which embraced both school and work. In the process, important, but hitherto unscripted issues, concerning discipline and resistance, control over labour processes, the hidden economy and not least, the routine sexism of working-class life, emerged in a way which allowed the students to give them proper weight.... (Cohen, 1984:143)

In all of this, Cohen was seeking to accomplish a number of purposes. He was concerned not so much with traditional vocational guidance, but with getting students "to question some of the 'taken-for-granted' aspects of leaving school." He was leading them to rethink what they assumed they already knew by "exploring new ways of representing what was already known." He was also giving them a new-found confidence in their own powers, by drawing upon their ideas and by explicitly linking what was to be learned with what was already known. In the words of the definition of relevance quoted elsewhere he had radically changed "the status of the learner in relation to what is being learned." Sawyer makes a similar point in regard to his Newfoundland experience of abandoning traditional approaches to social studies and instead using the community as a starting-point from which to move out into the world:

> ... once again, student-generated material was providing the 'text.' We used the information compiled by the groups for further investigation and as the basis for class discussion; their ideas and work, not the product of anonymous historians, was the heart of our study. By this time the class had begun to see this situation as natural, and the time and thoughtfulness reflected in some of the reports showed not only that they recognized their expanding role but also that they accepted the increased responsibility that went with it. (Sawyer, 1979:125)

Another example comes from the work of Bob Davis, a Toronto high-school teacher. He has described how he organized a unit on work for Grade 9 General Course (i.e., allegedly non-academic) students. He began by asking the students to list the jobs that they saw as most boring, most unhealthy, most exhausting and most stressful — a process that not only provided some indication of students' thinking but also provided a basis for discussion, particularly around the question of how the students formed their ideas (in many cases on the basis of television). From this, Davis moved to the learning of a list of necessary words, such as blue collar, white collar, strike, layoff, collective bargaining, and so on. As he puts it: "Students are expected to learn the meaning of these work terms.... They do a test on them. There is a common assumption by conservative critics of liberal school reform [I would add by some of the practitioners also — K.O.] that 'new curriculum' is just gazing at your navel and telling each other how it feels. In fact, the topic of 'work' has lots of precise knowledge connected with it, as much as any 'science'" (Davis, 1990:154). From these technical terms, Davis moved his students on to the Ontario Labour Code, with the aim of examining the legal rights of workers. That led into the question of unions and organizing, using the film *Maria* as a springboard for discussion. This, in turn, led to the singing and examination of work songs, some provided by Davis and others brought in by students. After all this, students were required to interview two workers, generally chosen from their relatives or other personal contacts, following a structured interview format. They then took up Studs Terkel's *Working* and wrote an imaginary personal story as though they were being interviewed by Terkel. This was followed by a visit to a workplace such as a General Motors assembly plant, and by further reading of Bill Freeman's novels about sailors and timber workers in nineteenth century Canada. The unit ended either with a pork-and-beans (traditional lumbermen's food) cookout for the whole school, or with a special presentation for parents, involving student talks, a film and a meal. This is a very bare summary of a rich and inventive unit that nicely illustrates the point made above about the necessity to combine teacher and student activity. Fortunately, Davis has described it in detail in an earlier book in this series and his account is worth examining closely.

The final example is taken from the work of Herb Kohl and describes a Grade 6 mathematics class. One of the students asked him what a number really was, and would not accept his conventional explanations that numbers were only abstractions, that "oneness" was the common quality of all groups that contained only one thing. Kohl's class told him that they knew this but it did not tell them what "one" really was. After much pondering, he decided to present the idea of mathematical models to the class in these terms:

> First I asked whether they could tell the difference between three dimes and two dimes, one book and six books. Of course they could, they said, and I explained that the intuitive sense of number came from dealing with experience and learning a language people created to deal with experience. I then asked if that language of number had to be true in every possible world, and Larry, our resident science fiction expert, said he could imagine a world where every time you put two objects together they turned into three. In that world there would be no two. Doris objected that there would still be the idea of two even if there were no two objects you could add up to two. Only the rules would have to be different. Adding would somehow have to have a statement like $1 + 1 = 3$. (Kohl, 1984:120)

At this point, Kohl told the students they were doing what mathematicians did, building models "that might sometimes fit our experience and at others fit experiences we could only imagine." He told them also that, though he could not explain what "one" was, he could show how mathematicians dealt with numbers. He used a series of cardboard boxes, arranged so that each box fitted into one bigger than it, with all the boxes fitting inside each other to make one big box, and from this he and the students devised a formula to explain the sequence. As in the other examples, students and teacher were working actively together to examine a problem of common interest, with the teacher having much to contribute and taking a directive, authoritative role in the lesson.The teacher did not silence the students by confronting them with an encyclopedic display of knowledge but rather stimulated them to think, explore and argue

Examples of other such classes may be found in past publications of *Our Schools/Our Selves*. They include a class investigation into the origin of words in Freinet (1990b: 78-81), the Miners' Handbook project of La maîtresse d'école (1989: 60-79), Elaine MacIntosh's project on Bears (OS/OS, I, 3 April '89: 41-54), and the Winnipeg–based Political Education Project's work on teaching politics to elementary school children (OS/OS, I, 2 Jan. 89: 133–143).

All these examples have certain points in common and serve to illustrate a particular kind of pedagogy, based upon these shared principles:

1. The teachers had a clearly articulated vision of education.
2. The material being taught was worthwhile and important; it was worth knowing.
3. The material was organized as a problem or issue to be investigated.
4. Careful and deliberate attention was given to the teaching of thinking, not as a set of isolated skills but in the context of valuable knowledge.
5. The teachers connected the material with students' knowledge and experience.
6. Students were required to become active in their own learning.
7. Students were encouraged to share, to build on each other's ideas.
8. Connections were established between the classroom and the world outside the school.
9. The classrooms were characterized by trust and openness so that students found it relatively easy to participate.

These nine principles have the power to make classrooms exciting and stimulating centres of worthwhile learning. They also draw upon, and indeed require, the enthusiasm, knowledge and skill of teachers, but in ways that depend upon and stimulate the enthusiasm, knowledge and skill of students. They make teaching and learning a collaborative process. They also have the potential to turn students into active, democratic citizens. They are indispensable to any theory of participatory, democratic citizenship, in which education and pedagogy must play a central part.

Chapter Four

The Elements Of Pedagogy For Democratic Clitizenship

This chapter forms the core of this book. To this point I have established (albeit briefly) the connection between education and citizenship, and argued that any useful theory of education, and therefore any useful political philosophy, must take account of pedagogy. I have described some recent developments in the theory and practice of pedagogy and, at the end of the last chapter, proposed nine elements that must be included in any pedagogy that aims at laying the foundations for democratic citizenship.

Before continuing, however, it might be worth saying a little more about citizenship, if only because it is not something that most people connect with teaching. Teachers, for example, tend to think of teaching in terms of techniques that work and techniques that do not. Teaching is what one does to show students how to solve quadratic equations, write a paragraph, operate a lathe, or learn whatever they are supposed to learn. Students think of teaching as those things that teachers do to help them, such as extending encouragement, taking an interest in them, giving them extra coaching, and making lessons interesting. Administrators and supervisors usually think of teaching in terms of covering the curriculum, obtaining respectable test scores, running an orderly classroom, and maintaining students' interest and cooperation. Parents want their children to be happy, to enjoy school, to learn something, and judge teaching accordingly. In all cases, teaching is defined and evaluated in terms of its impact within the classroom.

This is obviously important. It would make no sense for teachers to justify their teaching by saying that, although nothing is happening inside the classroom, results will show themselves in ten or fifteen years time. A teacher of science is expected to ensure that students actually learn some science; a music teacher has an obligation to give students an understanding and appreciation of music; and so for all other subjects in the curriculum. At the same time, teachers are usually expected to teach a variety of other things, such as good manners, tolerance, respect for other people, and so on. They share this responsibility with others, but they can never avoid it.

There is also another dimension to teaching, that in this book I describe as citizenship. In a thousand different ways, deliberately and accidentally, explicitly and implicitly, by example and by instruction, by what they say and do as well as by what they do not say and do, teachers help students to arrive at a way of seeing and interpreting the world. They teach them to be more or less active or passive, independent or submissive, cooperative or competitive, generous or selfish, trusting or fearful, and so on. And all these qualities have an impact on political life. They influence the extent to which students do or do not involve themselves in political life, both small-p and large-p. They influence the way they view and deal with other people, and thus shape the nature of neighbourhood, community and society at large.

My word for this is citizenship. All teachers teach it. They cannot avoid it. Every time they give an instruction, ask a question, deal with an interruption, take up an answer, make a comment, they are conveying a view of how the world works and how people should behave. Citizenship is not all those lessons on government in social studies classes. That is civics. Nor it is the singing of the national anthem or the celebration of ceremonial occasions. Those are patriotic exercises. Citizenship is far more than this. Citizenship is defined by the way we see the world around us, local, national and global, and by the part we choose to play in it.

In a society that claims to be democratic, citizenship is fundamentally important. Democracy, after all, means self-government, the rule of the people — and that means all the people, not just some of them. Democracy depends upon an ingrained commitment to freedom and equality, and on the willingness to work through the conflicts that arise between them. It involves respecting the rights of others. Above all, it means taking an active interest in the affairs of society. In Canada, however, the state of democratic citizenship leaves much to be desired. Canadian society continues to be characterized by unacceptable inequalities. Large groups of people are effectively excluded from the political process. For most Canadians, political involvement does not go beyond voting. As Philip Resnick puts it, Canada is a model liberal state, but it has some considerable way to go before it becomes truly democratic (Resnick, 1984). Our concept of democracy rests upon representation — the right to vote and to be represented — rather than upon participation. It is, therefore, hardly surprising that many Canadians report themselves to be disillusioned not just with their political leaders, but with the whole political process.

If we are to realize the potential of democratic citizenship, education has a vital role to play, as elites realized the moment that people won the right to vote. As the British politician, Robert Lowe, put it after the British working-class gained the right to vote in 1867: "... I believe it will be absolutely necessary to prevail on our future masters to learn their letters" (Winter, 1976:187). Education, in other words, was to be organized to ensure that newly enfranchised voters used their vote "responsibly," in order that the status quo would be disturbed as little as possible. Education for citizenship quickly became a very conservative activity.

At the same time, however, it contained the possibility of social change and transformation. Groups and individuals struggling for social change have always seen an ally in education, albeit an education that would itself need to be transformed. Socialist parties, labour unions, the women's movement, aboriginal people — all have seen education as a vital component of their struggle for social change.

If we are to use the potential of education for democratic citizenship we must pay attention both to curriculum and to pedagogy, to what we teach and how we teach it. This chapter deals particularly with how we should teach, if we wish to contribute to democratic citizenship. It consists of an examination of each of the nine elements of pedagogy that were listed at the end of the preceding chapter. Its purpose is to explain what must be included in any pedagogy that aims to lay the foundations for democratic citizenship.

1. Teachers Need A Clearly Articulated Vision Of Education

Good teachers possess a clear vision of education and of what it will do for their students. They are not simply technicians who take the prescribed curriculum, or the textbook, and work their students through it. They incorporate the curriculum into their philosophy of education and use what it has to offer in ways that make educational sense. This involves thinking carefully about goals and how to achieve them, and such thinking inevitably takes a teacher beyond the confines of the classroom. Educational goals do not exist in a vacuum. They emerge from thinking about what one wants for students and for the society in which they live. To plan to teach something, or to organize students so that they learn something, is to ask the question: why? Why should students have to learn this? What makes it justifiable or worthwhile? What purpose (or whose interests) are being served? Will the students or society at large be the better for it? Should they be learning something different? How will pedagogy influence what they learn? In this regard, the questions asked of the curriculum by critical pedagogy are useful.

There are those who reject this, arguing that all such questions are properly dealt with in the provincial curriculum and that the teacher's task is simply to teach what is contained in it as effectively as possible. Such, for example, was the argument of the Radwanski Report in Ontario, which called for a very tightly organized and controlled province-wide curriculum, with teachers having the freedom only to make instructional decisions about how best to teach it. At present, however, no provincial curriculum is this specific. Rather, curricula allow a good deal of flexibility to teachers. Even when curricula were more prescriptive, as in the days of external province-wide examinations, there was still considerable room for manoeuvre. There is no such thing as a teacher-proof curriculum. And even narrowly instructional decisions embody value-choices and reflect particular educational philosophies. Pedagogy is not neutral; it forms an important component of citizenship.

Therefore, teachers need a philosophy of education. They must be able to explain to themselves, and to their students (not to mention parents and administrators), why they are doing this rather than that, why these readings, these activities, these experiments, these tests, these topics — and so on — are worth doing. These questions can be answered only in the context of a conception of citizenship. What kind of persons do I want my students to be and to become? What kind of society do I want them to grow up in? How can they be equipped to take part in the continuing debate that is at the heart of any democratic society, and especially in Canada? How will my teaching do this?

These questions, and others like them, are not often asked in classrooms, where decisions tend to be of a much more narrowly technical nature, dealing with the hows but not the whys of teaching. The curriculum and the textbook are taken as givens and the task becomes how to prepare students for the test. The purpose of education becomes not worthwhile learning, but the accumulation of credits. Each unit of work becomes a stepping-stone to another unit, until enough have been covered to earn the necessary diploma. It is education not as learning but as credentialing, with the schools serving as society's employment agency.

For the most part, teachers see their work in student-centred, individualistic terms. They do not, by and large, see their work in any social or political context. They do not think in terms of citizenship as the word is used in these pages. Teachers see themselves as teachers of history or science or Grade 3 or special education, or whatever, with little reference to any broader context beyond the classroom.

Thus, teaching becomes a fundamentally conservative activity. Teachers are expected to do a better job within society as it exists, and not to ask questions about the very nature of that society, despite the fact that it exercises such a powerful influence in the classroom. Teachers become so locked into their particular tasks (in large part due to their working conditions,) that they have little time or inclination for thinking about the bigger picture. In the educational division of labour this is supposed to be the work of administrators, curriculum consultants and school trustees, and ministers of education, insofar as anyone thinks about it at all.

Thus, the system keeps moving with everyone involved too busy to wonder where it is going or why it should be going there. In this situation, teachers manage as best they can. There is no time to stand and stare, let alone to think, when there are always lessons to prepare, students to teach, work to mark and meetings to attend. Conservatism is entrenched.

However, education is not neutral. It cannot so easily be separated from politics. Public schooling, in particular, is inseparable from a conception of citizenship. It is not simply coincidence that many of the great names of educational theory are also the great names of political philosophy, such as Plato, Aristotle, Locke and Rousseau. It is also notable that many educational theorists, though not in the front rank of political philosophy, nonetheless thought carefully about social and political issues and linked education with them, among them the civic humanists of the Renaissance, the religious reformers of the Reformation, the rationalists of the Enlightenment, the nationalists of the nineteenth and twentieth centuries, and the democratic socialists of today.

Educational theory and political theory are inseparably connected and the connection is provided by citizenship. A theory of citizenship leads to a theory of education, and a theory of education provides the criteria by which to judge the worthwhileness of what is to be taught and how. Reflecting on his Newfoundland experience, Don Sawyer put it this way:

> A classroom is a microcosmic society; what you see is what you teach, and what you say is a lot less important than what you do. If you believe in the principles of democracy and humanism you had better operate a democratic, humane classroom or you are contradicting those values. Likewise, if you believe in the integrity of the individual and the acceptance of differences, but use punishment and reward to coerce students into compliance with your views and needs, you are teaching the need for submission and conformity. (Sawyer, 1979:73)

To say that good teaching springs from a clearly articulated vision of education, however, takes us only so far. The vision must not only be clearly articulated; it must also be intellectually and morally defensible. A racist could have an extremely clear vision of society and education, but it is a vision that should not be allowed to influence education. A vision of education must be able to meet the tests traditionally associated with education. Intellectually, it must respect factual evidence, be open to critical revision, and incorporate the principles of reasoned inquiry and debate. Morally, it must meet the tests of fairness and justice, respect the rights of individuals and promote democratic principles.

It is dangerously easy to get lost in the swamp of educational theory. Nonetheless, teachers need some set of principles if they are to distinguish between what is pedagogically worthwhile and what is not, especially if their teaching is to foster citizenship. These principles can conveniently be thought of as the eight C's: Country-specific (or Canadian); Cosmopolitan; Caring; Critical; Creative; Coherent; Cooperative and Committed. These serve as a short-hand way of evaluating curricula, materials and pedagogy, even when immersed in the hurly-burly of teaching, with little time to become philosophically sophisticated.

The *country-specific* or *Canadian* principle recognizes the obvious fact that citizenship does not exist on its own, but is a product of time and place. In Canada especially, democratic citizenship means being able to take part in the continuing debate as to what kind of society we are and wish to be. Bilingualism, multiculturalism, federalism and regionalism, all ensure that Canadian citizenship cannot be some fixed entity, carved in stone forever. Moreover, citizenship as a reality, and not simply a legal fiction, is a matter of struggle and conflict, as various groups such as women and aboriginal people fight for full citizenship rights. So students must be familiar with the continuing debate over citizenship in Canada, both historically and in the present, and must also be able to participate in it. This is what is meant by saying that there is a country–specific or Canadian dimension to education.

At the same time, education and citizenship must be viewed in *cosmopolitan* terms. Old-fashioned, exclusive nationalism, nineteenth-century style, is dangerous and destructive. Students must think in global terms. The concept of spaceship earth must become a reality, not just a cliché. This is not inconsistent with the Canadian dimension of education. Canada is not a nation-state in the standard nineteenth century sense, in which "... the ideological demands of one cultural group or nation are forced upon all other groups within its borders." (Cook, 1987:5) Canadians, perhaps more than most people, are aware of diversity and able to distinguish between unity and uniformity. The ability to reconcile different levels of identity — personal, local, national and global — will be increasingly important in the world of the future. Our students must therefore be able to identify themselves as both Canadians and cosmopolitans, or members of the global community.

They must also be *caring* people, and their education should help them to care in two senses: first, to care for people and, second, to care for the planet on which we all live. Neither needs much explanation. Caring for people means being tolerant, treating others as ends not means, thinking in terms of brotherhood and sisterhood. Thus, racism, sexism and any form of prejudice have to be eliminated as destructive of community. Caring for the environment is obviously also important. We have become increasingly aware of the seriousness of the environmental problems facing us and, though much more slowly, we are beginning to realize that if these problems are to be solved we will have to change the way we live.

This also means being *critical*, not in the sense of being endlessly negative or resorting to a knee-jerk cynicism, but in the straightforward sense of learning to think rationally for ourselves. Students must learn the habits of constructive scepticism (which is very different from mindless cynicism) if they are to withstand the manipulation to which we are all increasingly subject. They must know how to assess an argument, how to separate fact from interpretation, and how to use all the other elements of critical thinking.

At the same time, they must be encouraged to be *creative*. Everyone has the potential to be creative in some way, and creativity is an essential aspect of living, be it expressed through music, gardening, sport, work or some other manner. It is not restricted to a small minority, and it is certainly something that must be encouraged in everyone through education.

Students must also be *coherent*. They must be able to communicate clearly and effectively. This requires an ability to read, write, listen, and speak with purpose and assurance, preferably in more than one language.The experience of acquiring or using a second language is often a better preparation to solving problems in communicating in one's own tongue than all the direct teaching in the world.

Finally, students must be *cooperative* and *committed*. The first needs no explanation except to make the point that cooperation must replace competition as the organizing principle of social life. Not only is it satisfying in itself, but it is the way to mutual survival in the world in which our students will spend their lives. Commitment means a commitment to action and involvement, to shaping one's life according to the principles listed here. Both education and citizenship are about living and acting, not merely thinking and reflecting.

The eight C's then, are an attempt, in simple and simplified form, to represent the kind of vision of education that shapes pedagogy. Other formulations are possible. The fundamental point is that teachers make the connection between citizenship and pedagogy and locate their teaching in a worthwhile vision of what education and society should become.

2. The Material To Be Taught Must Be Worthwhile And Important; It Must Be Worth Knowing

Teaching students can be like climbing a mountain — it is done simply because they are there. What is to be taught is laid out in the curriculum or the textbook and the teacher's task becomes one of getting students to learn it, or at least to remember it long enough to be tested on it. As a result, students are often expected to learn long lists of facts that mean little or nothing to them. History becomes a recital of causes, events and results; science a series of formulas and definitions; literature a parade of author's names, characters and stylistic devices; and so on. The facts that are taught are not put into any broader context or in any way linked to students' experience.

The classic example of this kind of teaching is to be found in Charles Dickens' description of Gradgrind Academy, in *Hard Times*. There, Mr. Gradgrind was quizzing a class of young children and asked one of them, Sissy Jupe, what a horse was. Sissy had grown up with horses in the circus, but Mr. Gradgrind did not want to know about that, nor did he let her talk about it. He wanted a precise definition of a horse and when Sissy could not give him one, he turned to a boy in the class and got what to him was a perfect answer: "... Quadruped Graminivorous. Forty teeth, namely twenty-four grinders, four eye-teeth, and twelve incisive. Sheds coat in spring; in marshy countries, sheds hoofs too. Hoofs hard, but requiring to be shod with iron, age known by marks in mouth." The answer was obviously satisfactory: "... Now, girl number twenty," said Mr. Gradgrind, "you know what a horse is." For Mr. Gradgrind believed in facts. As he told the teacher: "... Now, what I want is, Facts. Teach these boys and girls nothing but Facts. Facts alone are wanted in life. Plant nothing else, and root out everything else. You can only form the minds of reasoning animals upon Facts...." And the teacher, Mr. M'Choakumchild was of like mind:

> He, and some hundred and forty other schoolmasters, had been lately turned at the same time, in the same factory, on the same principles, like so many pianoforte legs. He had been put

> through an immense variety of paces, and had answered volumes of heart-breaking questions. Orthography, etymology, syntax, and prosody, biography, astronomy, geography, and general cosmography, the sciences of compound proportion, algebra, land surveying and levelling, social music, and drawing from models, were all at the ends of his ten chilled fingers. He knew all about all the Water Sheds of all the world (whatever they are), and all the histories of all the peoples, and all the names of all the rivers and mountains, and all the productions, manners, and customs of all the countries, and all their boundaries and bearings on the two-and-thirty points of the compass.

Dickens' comment on this story of dead knowledge is telling: "... Ah! rather overdone, M'Choakumchild. If he had only learnt a little less, how infinitely better he might have taught much more!"

In contrast, in the examples of good teaching presented in the previous chapter, the teachers were all concerned to organize the facts in their lessons in ways that would enrich their students' understanding. Facts were used to raise questions, to suggest concepts, to illustrate issues, all of which had some connection with life and living and were not only of textbook importance.

Concerning what questions, concepts and issues are important enough to teach to students, one can identify two extreme positions. One is represented by the nineteenth century poet and critic — and school inspector — Matthew Arnold, and his twentieth century descendants, who insist that everyone should learn "the best that has been known and thought," in literature, in music, in art, in history and so on. What is best is that which has been acknowledged by tradition and convention and by the best minds through the ages. Arnold himself valued the best that has been known and thought because it gives us a set of ideals against which to judge what he called "the stock of received notions." This critical dimension of knowledge, that sees it as a test for deciding what is acceptable in life and what is not, is sometimes ignored by Arnold's supporters and critics, who see him as concerned only that everyone memorizes their Shakespeare and sings along with Mozart. He was also much criticized in his lifetime for neglecting the importance of science and for looking only to the past for guidance. There is strength in all such criticisms, as there is also in Raymond Williams' condemnation of Arnold's class-biased view of what counts as culturally valuable (Williams, 1961:120-136), but nonetheless, Arnold makes a vital point. There is a store of knowledge built up over human history that education should preserve and pass on to each generation, while at the same time submitting it to critical reflection.

At the other extreme from Arnold is the view of knowledge that rejects any idea of absolutes or eternals. This view sees knowledge as a reflection of political and social power. If some knowledge is treated as superior or assigned a higher status, it is not because it is inherently better in any way but rather because it is sanctioned by those with power and influence. Ballet and opera, for example, are publicly subsidized while country music is not, not because they are higher forms of artistic expression but because they were historically the entertainment of the upper classes and still retain their support. Accordingly, Arnold's notion of "the best that has been known and thought" must be exposed as the disguised expression of class interest, hiding political and social inequality under a cloud of allegedly impartial artistic judgment. In terms of the curriculum, Arnold's position is seen as denying the validity of students' own culture (be it native, working–class, ethnic or something else) and justifying the cultural values of the old European aristocracy. Such, at least, in very simple outline is the argument of the sociologists of knowledge who turned their attention to the curriculum in the 1970's (Young, 1971). Worthwhile knowledge, in this view, is to be found not in the classics, nor in the accumulated experience of humanity, but in students' needs and interests. The teacher's job is not to impose knowledge on students from the outside, but to listen to students and to help them formulate what it is they want to do.

These are the extreme positions, and obviously there are many others between them. One that has emerged in recent years is associated with E. D. Hirsch and his concept of "cultural literacy" (Hirsch, 1988). Hirsch sees culture, not in the sense of the classics or of the literary canon, but as a shared way of life. Such a way of life, he argues, if it is to be shared, must arise from a set of common ideas, symbols, references, i.e. a common body of knowledge. This body of knowledge becomes especially important at a time of high immigration when new citizens bring with them knowledge new to the society to which they come without necessarily being familiar with the knowledge on which the society is built. Cultural literacy is a kind of social cement, binding people together through a set of familiar references covering all aspects of life. For example, if people do not know what is meant by such phrases as "the first time since Confederation," or "so-and-so struck out," or "who do you think you are? Einstein?" (and so on), they will be unable to understand and therefore to take part in society. Their citizenship will be diminished by their cultural illiteracy.

Hirsch's views have been attacked as a reactionary attempt to protect white, middle-class, male power from the new demands of a multi-cultural society. In education, he has been criticized for advocating a cook-book approach to curriculum, equating education with the learning of approved facts, drawn from the lists he has compiled of the essential contents of cultural literacy. There is a certain point to these criticisms, and especially to the first, but it is difficult to deny the central premise of his argument, that a society depends upon the possession of a body of shared knowledge that makes argument and debate possible. This is especially the case in Canada, where we are so heavily influenced by American culture that American myths, symbols and points of reference swamp their Canadian equivalents and where, as a result, there is a constant risk that we will end up seeing ourselves through American eyes. The driving force of the Canadian Studies movement in education was "to know ourselves," and if we are to be concerned with Canadian citizenship, we cannot dismiss the question of knowledge, which I have discussed in another book in this series (Osborne, 1988).

The question of precisely what knowledge is worthwhile and important has led to much discussion on the left of the development of a working-class curriculum. The argument is made that the traditional academic curriculum has not worked for most working-class students and that, even when it has, it represents a type of cultural imposition, denying the validity of working-class culture and attempting to replace it with middle-class values and ideals. Thus, the argument goes, working-class students should be offered a curriculum that respects their culture and values. This analysis is not accepted by all on the left, some of whom see any attempt to develop a uniquely working-class curriculum as leading to a ghettoization of working-class students and to their exclusion from important and valuable aspects of human experience.

Connell, for example, proposes a middle ground, arguing that neither the traditional academic curriculum nor some new working-class curriculum is acceptable, but that what we need is a combination of the two approaches:

> It proposes that working-class kids get access to formal knowledge *via* learning which begins with their own experience and the circumstances which shape it but does not stop there.... It draws on existing school knowledge and on what working-class people know already, and organizes this selection of information around problems such as economic survival and collective action, handling the disruption of households, unemployment, responding to the impact of new technology, managing problems of personal identity and association, understanding how schools work and why. (Connell, 1982:199-200)

There is nothing to object to in any of this, but it is incomplete. It wrongly restricts working-class knowledge to problems of immediate and personal concern. We must, however, while not ignoring these, always seek to go beyond them. Working-class students, like any others, have a good deal to learn from history, literature and the arts, that are as much part of their heritage as anyone else's. The problem with the so-called "academic" curriculum, so often criticized by educational theorists on the left, is not that it is academic, for it rarely is, usually consisting rather of a drudging march through lists of dead facts. The problem lies much more with how it is organized and taught. Bill Hannan is surely correct when he writes: "... We do need a good analysis of our heritage and working-class culture. We do also need to keep in mind that we are not merely trying to implant a different class culture. But I don't like thinking of the present division as a choice of alternatives. A democratic curriculum will be a synthesis of these conflicting class cultures" (Hannan, 1985:285).

All of which leaves the question: what are the criteria by which teachers can decide whether what the knowledge they teach is worthwhile and important? More than a century ago Herbert Spenser suggested this approach to worthwhile knowledge. First and most important was knowledge aiding in self-preservation, such as health, physiology and nutrition. Second came knowledge aimed at earning a living. Third was knowledge to prepare students for future parenthood. Fourth was preparation for citizenship. Fifth and last came knowledge for the "miscellaneous refinements of life," such as art and literature. Spencer based his proposals on an analysis of what he saw as necessary for the physical survival of the individual and of society, but he did not go far enough. We need to think of education for citizenship in terms that go beyond mere survival. Education, like citizenship, must be directed towards the extension of participatory democracy, cooperation and social justice, and thus towards social change.

This brings us to some criteria of worthwhileness and importance. When asking themselves the question, why is it important to teach something and why is it important to teach it in any particular way, teachers should consider these principles. First, students should be helped to understand their world in a truly critical sense, so that they do not simply adapt to it or learn how to manipulate it, but so that they can see it as it is and also see it as it might be, and gain the skills and dispositions to progress from one to the other. Second, education should help students to gain control over their own lives, by learning to think for themselves, by learning the skills needed for economic survival, and by learning how to participate in the sociopolitical process. Third, education should equip students with the knowledge, skills and disposition to work for social change. Fourth, it should give them a sense of solidarity and community with others, locally, nationally and globally, so that they learn to work cooperatively with others and understand how their actions affect them. Fifth, education should help students live rich, many-faceted lives so that they can choose how they wish to live. All five principles imply that students should learn not only about the here-and-now and the immediately relevant, but also about the wider human heritage of which they are both inheritors from generations past and the trustees for the generations to come. If pedagogy can satisfy these five criteria, then it will play an important role in producing an active and democratic citizenship.

3. Material To Be Taught Should Be Organized And Presented As Problems Or Issues To Be Investigated

To speak of organizing pedagogy around problems or issues is *not* to argue for exercises completed through tests and worksheets that are confined to the low-level gathering of factual information. Such exercises are not so much aids to learning as obstacles to it: hurdles more or less arbitrarily erected by the teacher to see how many students will stumble or fall. They emphasize not understanding but short-term memory of facts, as students understand very well when they ask the question, "Will this be on the test?" If it will, they will pay some attention to it; if it won't, they will ignore it. Understanding is sacrificed for coverage. The priority becomes not that students develop a rich, contextual understanding of a series of topics, but that they cover a curriculum from beginning to end.

Such exercises discover only whether students have acquired knowledge of a certain topic, not whether they can use it. This distinction between acquiring and using knowledge is important, for it is obvious that knowledge that is neither used nor seen as useful has a very short life. It is retained for a specific purpose, usually passing a test or an examination, and then quickly forgotten. Oakes and Lipton describe the distinction this way (Oakes & Lipton, 1990:85):

> This separation between acquiring knowledge and using knowledge dictates that schools teach small facts and skills rather than large concepts. It causes children to be engaged in

> passive, low-level thinking rather than high-level thinking. The separation promotes superficial coverage of a wide array of topics and skills over a deep understanding of fewer, more central ideas. The typical curriculum bears little resemblance to the spontaneous, high-energy experience-gathering and problem-solving that children do so naturally. It is quite unlike the real, problem-solving worlds of managing households, succeeding in the workplace, and making democratic decisions.

This does not mean that if we are to teach *via* issues and problems we must select only problems that are of current, immediate, personal relevance to students of the "How do I deal with my parents?" variety. Such a curriculum would be unacceptably limited, condescending to students and quite inadequate for the kind of citizenship that is being advocated in this book.

The problems and issues that students must learn to think about, and do in fact enjoy thinking about, are those that embody the central concepts of life, such as justice, community, rights, duties, goodness and so on. If, following the philosopher Michael Oakeshott, we think of human experience over time as a great and continuing conversation, then our task as teachers is to introduce students to it and initiate them into it so that they will be in time able to contribute to it, to extend and redirect it.

This involves acquiring knowledge, certainly, but it also means that the knowledge must be used, and by initiating students into the great human conversation, they will see it as useful and they will come to use it. The central questions are as old as Plato: What is the good life? What is the good society? What is the good citizen? What is the appropriate balance between the private interest and the public good; between cooperation and competition; between liberty and equality; between majority and minority rights; between justice and order; between authority and freedom? What do these words mean anyway? How do they reflect themselves in specific contexts, such as abortion, censorship, native rights, constitutional change, privatization, immigration, social reform and so on? To deal satisfactorily with such questions means to be able to understand them, to think about them, to listen critically to a range of viewpoints, to reach a decision, and to act. And this means acquiring, but above all using, knowledge. To quote another philosopher, this time Isaiah Berlin (Yudkin, 1971:10):

> Unless men (*sic*) are given the chance to find out what kind of world they live in, what they have made, are making, and could make of it — and this can only be done if they have some notion of what other men are thinking and teaching and doing, and how and why — they will continue to walk in darkness and be faced by the unpredicted and sometimes appalling consequences of one another's activities...

To which, if citizenship is to be complete, we should add the words of Marx, when he noted that philosophers have concerned themselves only with understanding the world, when the real task is to change it.

To accomplish this, pedagogy will be important, though obviously not all-powerful, since it will need to be reinforced by the curriculum content (see Osbsorne, 1989), the overall organization and climate of the classroom and the school, but it nonetheless will play its part. Above all, it must concentrate on helping students to use the knowledge they acquire, rather than remember it as a bundle of miscellaneous facts, in the style of Trivial Pursuit.

This means seeing knowledge as important (since it is needed to secure the full power of citizenship) not because it is there and therefore must be learned, but because it has the power to illuminate the central issues of human life, both individual and social. It is not static, but dynamic, in the sense that it should be seen as open to challenge and to question. Obviously we must teach students to respect facts and evidence; knowledge must not be treated as a convenience, though it often is.

If knowledge is to be used in this way, however, pedagogy becomes important. Knowledge must be presented to students not as a solid mountain of fact to be scaled, but because it throws light on the central issues of our time. We must follow the advice of the historian, Alan Bullock, who wrote that, pedagogically, we must begin "... not from the achievements of the past, but from the human needs of young people today" (Bullock, 1985:186-7). As Bullock points out, this is not mere trendy relevance:

> But it is the same role which the rediscovery of the ancient world played for the Renaissance, providing those who were young then with a strange and exciting world which they could explore and on which they could draw to work out their own answers to the questions and conflicts presented by their own experience. Today the material on which to draw is no longer limited to the ancient world, but includes the whole range of human experience, contemporary as well as historical, that of other cultures as well as our own Western tradition.

To see what this means in practice, we need only think back to the examples described towards the end of the previous chapter. The point of using the Industrial Revolution to illustrate the concept of time and the place it occupies in contemporary life is precisely to encourage students to use and not simply to acquire knowledge. This can be done by linking some fairly conventional historical subject-matter with a question of social importance in a way that students can understand and to which they can contribute. The same process can be seen at work in Bob Davis's unit on work. In both cases, it would have been easy to saturate students with lists of names, dates, inventions, time-lines, and all the other trappings of traditional history teaching. In both cases, this approach was deliberately rejected as anti-educational, for it would have done nothing for the development of students' powers of thought, the extension of their knowledge, their faith in their own powers as thinkers and learners, or their commitment to education. I learned this the hard way very early in my teaching career. As a student teacher in an English working-class district, I was given a small group of fifteen-year-old boys who were waiting (itching might be a better word) to leave school to work in the nearby car factories. Since they were only putting in time, I was told to do whatever I wanted with them. I knew immediately what I wanted to do. I had just obtained my history degree, I was (and remain) intensely committed to the subject, I had made a special study of English labour history. What could be better than to give these boys a short course in the history of unions, since they were (a) from the working class and (b) going to work in a car factory that was completely unionized and often in the news for the activities of its shop-stewards and frequent strikes. So I presented a short history course. It was, on paper, reasonably interesting; it was, again on paper, relevant; it contained a lot of knowledge. My students tolerated me with more or less polite boredom. It quickly became obvious that, for them, I was simply one more pointless, even if friendly and sympathetic, part of the price they had to pay to leave school. Shortly afterwards, in another school, again in a district dominated by the automobile industry, I was asked by a livelier group why I wanted to teach anyway. It wasn't man's work, they insisted, nor did it pay well. Why not join them in the car plant when they left school? I gave them a conventional answer and carried on with my conventional course, which they resisted with considerable force. I quickly came to realize that I had things backwards. I was trying to get students to acquire knowledge. They saw no use for it, except to pass a test (and they did not care about passing anyway, since they knew there were jobs waiting for them), and I did not make it useful by linking it to anything beyond itself. My pedagogy was hopelessly out of place in the context in which I was teaching.

To make the point even more clearly, consider this example. The task set for the teacher was to teach a class of twelve–to–thirteen–year-olds about the Greek city-states. How easy it would have been to prepare a worksheet, work the class through the textbook (including the end-of-chapter questions), throw in a filmstrip or two, and give them a test. Somewhat more imaginatively, he might have included some primary sources, a bit of role-playing, some modelling, and any other kind of activity-based learning. It would be kinder than the first version, but it would do nothing more for the students' development. They would still be the recipients, though probably more willingly, of inert knowledge. Instead, consider the approach actually taken. First, the teacher asked himself the question: How can I turn the Greek city-state into a vehicle for worthwhile learning, such that (1) the students obtain the necessary information; (2) it helps them reflect upon and extend what they already know; (3) it enables them to contribute to the process of learning so that it involves them working collaboratively with each other and their teacher; and (4) it can be connected in some way with an important aspect of the human experience. The teacher's answer was as follows: the city-state is an example of community; the students themselves live in a community; the issue of community is important and, provided it is phrased in suitable language, is one that students can discuss. In fact, it raises interesting questions: What is a community, anyway? What makes a collection of people a community? How important is a sense of community for people? Where does one draw the line between the public and the private spheres? Is the school a community? Should it be? Can it be made so? What about the neighbourhood? The city? And so on.

On this basis, the lesson proceeded. Things began with the teacher asking the students if they knew what a hermit was. Some did, and so the lesson moved ahead. It would not have mattered if no-one had known; the teacher could have provided the information. Some of the more bizarre examples were presented to arouse curiosity, most notably St. Simeon Stylites with his forty years of living on top of a tall column to prove his faith and devotion. The students were asked if they would like to be hermits. If so, why? If not, why not? Why did most people choose to live in some sort of group? What were the pro's and con's? What kinds of groups could the students think of? They named clans, tribes, villages, clubs, families and on and on. There was nothing very flashy about the teaching techniques: The teacher prodded, asked questions, provided some instruction here and there, summarized points on the blackboard, but the students provided the ideas. Their responses built on each other; they fleshed out each other's answers; they challenged each other at times; they asked questions out of genuine puzzlement; they did not allow the teacher simply to have his own way. On this basis, the more general questions were introduced: What is a community? Is a football crowd a community? A rock-concert audience? How important is it for people to feel a sense of community? What about the school? The neighbourhood? These questions were not so much answered, as identified and tentatively explored. They set the scene for looking at the Greek city-states of Athens and Sparta, as historical examples of communities. What was the influence of geographical size? Of the size of the population? Could one speak of a community when women and slaves were excluded? How were citizens produced? How does a community reproduce itself over time?

These and other questions made it possible to deal with Athens and Sparta thoroughly and in a way the students found attractive for the most part. They were not only acquiring knowledge, they were using it and, in the process, rethinking what they already knew. They discovered that they knew a lot more than they realized. They were not empty vessels being filled up or clean slates being written on, they were actively producing knowledge. Their teacher had done them the courtesy of assuming that they knew something. Finally, the topic concluded by comparing Athens and Sparta with the city and neighbourhood in which the students lived. Did they feel a sense of community? Could it be strengthened? Should it be and, if so, how? The same questions were asked of the school. And, in the process, the eight C's, described above, were all included. This example illuminates two other points. One, students can do far more than we usually realize; and two, pedagogical process is not so much problem-solving as problem-posing and exploring. Both points need some short clarification.

So far as the first is concerned, it is important not to accept too readily the arguments of some developmental psychologists, particularly those who follow some version of Piaget's theories and who distinguish among pre-operational, concrete and abstract thinking. This is not the place to discuss developmental psychology in any detail but, in barest outline, the argument is that young children's thinking is illogical, haphazard and dominated by immediate experience. As they move through childhood and into adolescence, children's thinking becomes more organized and coherent, though it is limited to what is concrete and tangible. Only by high school do most students begin to think abstractly, about ideas and hypotheses. This is the pattern, for example, contained in Bruner's sequence of enactive, iconic and symbolic reasoning. In the first, children understand and explain things by acting upon them, by demonstration and physical movement; in the second, they are able to do so through visual images and representations (hence iconic); in the third, they can do so through abstract symbols such as equations or words. Peel makes a similar point when he speaks of pre-logical, describer and explainer thinking. In the first, children's explanations are haphazard and irrational by adult standards. In the second, they can describe events but not explain them. The ability to explain (to use the formula, "if x... then y"; to set up hypotheses; to control variables; and so on) develops only in the midteens (Osborne, 1975).

Such at least are the conclusions of much developmental psychology as applied to teaching. They have led to some wrong-headed conclusions that have done a disservice to students. The basic formulation is obviously reasonable: the ability to reason logically and abstractly develops over time. There is a general sequence of pre-logical through concrete to abstract thinking. From this basic truth, however, unduly pessimistic conclusions have been drawn, to the effect that students can hardly think at all. However, the research is not as straightforward and simple as it sometimes appears, and its conclusions are open to some question. Its findings have been largely overgeneralized. Simply because students are thinking concretely in one subject does not mean that they must think the same way in all others. Nor is their experience limited only to the directly personal. As Egan points out, even young children know something of fear, love, jealousy and other such "abstractions," that provide a rich connection with the record of human experience generally (Egan, 1983). Even when students do demonstrate concrete thinking, this does not mean that they can do no other. Concrete thinking may well be the result of previous teaching. If, for example, students have not been accustomed by their teachers to think in abstract ways, it is not surprising that they do not do so on a psychologist's test. Moreover, it is difficult if not impossible to separate thoughts from words, and assessments of thinking can be unduly influenced by proficiency with words. Thus, middle-class students (who, in any case, are often more able to play the school game) may easily appear to be more advanced thinkers than their working-class counterparts.

Teachers should therefore be very sceptical of claims as to what students can or cannot understand. It is too easy to deny students access to abstract ideas on the spurious ground that they are not ready for them or cannot handle them. It is, of course, true that they will not understand abstractions if they are taught abstractly. It is obviously pointless to teach academic philosophy to ten-year-olds. But this is very different from saying that ten-year-olds cannot in their own way handle philosophical issues. They ask philosophical questions all the time. They are intensely interested in purposes and causes and, in one form of another, are always asking the question, why? Indeed, Matthew Lipman and his colleagues have shown beyond any doubt that philosophy can be taught in the elementary school (Lipman *et al.*, 1977). The task is not to avoid abstractions but to teach them in concrete ways, that draw on experiences familiar to students, that connect with what they already know and lead them to go beyond it, as in the example of the Greek city-state.

The point is that the central issues of human experience can be approached by students, even in the elementary school. To teach in ways that address these issues is not something that has to be left to high school or university. Even so-called slow students can do it. Indeed, when given the chance they often prove not to be so slow after all. Not only are the central issues accessible to everyone, and important in any worthwhile conception of citizenship, they have the advantage of adding an element of interest and relevance to conventional school-work.

At the same time it must be stressed that not every lesson or every topic needs to bear the burden of reflection and problem-posing. There are times when experience should be its own reward; a story, a poem, a painting, an experiment, a song, will often stand alone. All too often the experience of a poem or a story is spoiled by the questions that inevitably follow it. A high school student once told me he enjoyed *Crime ent* the first time he read it. Even a second read- . too bad, but the third and fourth readings, accom- ..d by all the notes and questions on theme and plot and symbolism and characterization, were more than he could stand. Our pedagogy should address the central issues of experience in cumulatively reinforcing ways, but we should not drum them into the heads of students in every single lesson.

Nor, to return to the second implication of the city-state example, should we be so arrogant as to think in terms of straightforward problem-solving. The central issues of experience, the big questions of individual and social life, have been with us since social life began. They will be with us as long as it lasts. They cannot be "solved", except by the use of coercive power, benevolent or otherwise, which is no solution at all. They have to be lived with, examined, re–examined and pondered. Our answers must necessarily be tentative and provisional. In pedagogical terms we are concerned with opening students' minds not closing them, with teaching them to identify the questions and explore the answers but, in the final analysis, to arrive at their own answers. Thus when Oakes and Lipton write that "... children do their best school learning when they use new knowledge to solve real problems" (Oakes & Lipton, 1990:81), it is too simple a statement. The "real" problems of citizenship (as opposed to problems of the order of whether to join the choir or the soccer team) are too complex for conventional solutions, at least in any democratic society. It makes more sense to speak, with Freire, of problem-posing than of problem-solving. We are initiating students into the great conversation, not teaching them to close it down once and for all.

In this connection, the Club of Rome some years ago made a valuable distinction between what is called maintenance learning and innovative learning. The former is what we mostly do today and consists of teaching "fixed outlooks, methods and roles for dealing with known and recurring situations." It is education as problem-solving, based on the assumption that the problems are familiar and can be dealt with by precedent and tradition. While useful, such an approach is, on its own, inadequate and must be accompanied by innovative learning, that consists of anticipating and identifying problems and finding new ways to deal with them, since they are unlikely to be the same as those we have known. This is not so much problem-solving as problem-posing; it is "a necessary means of preparing individuals and societies to act in concert in new situations" (Botkin *et al.*, 1979:43). In outline, the two approaches can be compared as follows:

Maintenance Learning	Innovative Learning
Problem-solving	Problem-formulating
Value-conserving	Value-creating
Adaptation	Anticipation
Following leaders	Participation
Emphasis on past	Focus on future
Conformity	Autonomy
Learning facts	Critical judgment
Analysis	Integration
Emphasis on the national	Emphasis on the global

It is not a question of abandoning the former for the latter, but of combining the two so that the latter receives more emphasis than it does now. The examples presented in this book all show how it might be done.

4. Careful And Deliberate Attention Must Be Given To The Teaching of Thinking

If democratic citizenship is a key educational goal, then it follows that students must be able to use the skills that they will need as citizens. If they are to be personally empowered, socially engaged, able to deal with issues of political and social importance, they must above all be able to think clearly for themselves and to act upon the results of their thinking.

Fortunately, this priority is also rooted in the age-long educational tradition that stresses the importance of clear thinking.

Although the educational literature is full of discussion about critical thinking and its related skills, the research evidence suggests that we have not been very successful in teaching students to think. We have, it seems, spent much more time in teaching students factual knowledge, than we have in teaching them intellectual skills. Anyone who takes the time to look at tests and examinations, both past and present, will quickly find that they emphasize the remembering of information far more than they do analyzing and manipulating it. Where schools have taught skills, they have concentrated on the basic skills associated with the 3R's, and on the social skills involved in living and working with other people. These are obviously important and necessary, but what has been neglected is helping students to think for themselves, as they must if they are to enjoy the rights and responsibilities of democratic citizenship.

Thinking for oneself has something to do with what people in education usually call critical thinking, which has attracted renewed attention in recent years. It has various definitions, but perhaps the most useful is that provided by Harvey Siegel, who defines critical thinking as being "appropriately moved by reasons" (Siegel, 1988). In offering this definition, Siegel makes the point that thinking is much more than a list of skills that a person can decide to use, or not to use, in any given situation. Critical thinking, in other words, involves much more than knowing how to use a set of debating tricks, or knowing how to demolish an argument. It is both a set of skills and a disposition to act. It means at all times shaping one's views and actions according to the best evidence available, according to rational principles. In other words, critical thinking is not merely a method for analyzing and spotting flaws in what other people say and do; it is a set of principles for shaping one's own life, both in thought and action. This is what Richard Paul calls critical thinking in the strong sense, as opposed to seeing it simply as a set of academic exercises to be learned and deployed, which he calls critical thinking in the weak sense (Paul, 1989).

This view of critical thinking has obvious implications for teaching, not least in its message that thinking is not just something that teachers teach to their students, but also something that they model and demonstrate in all that they do. This is also borne out by the research on the teaching of thinking, that points to three general conclusions concerning what we must do if we are to teach students to think effectively. First, we must be very clear about what it is that we want them to do. Second, we must ensure that thinking is emphasized consistently in all subjects and grade levels. Third, thinking must be embedded in the very context of schooling, in the rules and expectations of the school, its evaluation and reporting policies, in all aspects of the so-called hidden curriculum. These three conclusions can be summarized as clarity, consistency and context, and they are worth further discussion.

So far as clarity is concerned, theorists and researchers are unanimous that the teaching of thinking has often suffered because teachers were not clear enough about just what it was they were trying to teach. Thinking, after all, is a deceptive word: we all think we know what it means and thus see no need to further define it. In reality, however, unless we are clear what it is, it is difficult to teach it properly. It is dangerously easy to assume that thinking is somehow inevitably contained in subject matter, so that, for example, when students study a mathematical equation, or learn how to analyze a poem, they are also learning how to think. Thus, tests and examinations often contain questions beginning with the word "discuss," that are supposed to trigger thinking but, in reality, rarely do.

There now exist many useful analyses of what is involved in critical thinking, and there is not space here to describe them. Fortunately, they are easily available (Ennis, 1962; Paul, 1989; Beyer, 1988), and they are all elaborations of the basic steps described by Dewey and discussed earlier in Chapter 2: identifying a problem; collecting and assessing information; arriving at a tentative solution to the problem; analyzing that solution in terms of its logical consistency, of its consistency with the evidence, and in terms of its desirability and practicality. Each of these steps obviously involves further abilities.

They include, for example, the ability to detect errors in logic and reasoning, the ability to assess evidence for credibility and reliability, the ability to locate information, and so on. The various elaborations of critical thinking now available all provide detailed specifications and make it easily possible for teachers to work out their own models of thinking. Whatever the details of any particular model, the central point is that, if we are to teach students to think effectively, we must be clear — and, equally important, so must they — about what this means.

Once clarity has been achieved, and a useful teaching model established, it becomes important that critical thinking is taught in all subjects and grade levels. It is obviously not something that should be done only in certain contexts. It must permeate the whole curriculum, beginning in the very early years. As noted earlier, Lipman has demonstrated that philosophy can be taught even to elementary schoolchildren. It is not necessary, nor is it really possible, to design a sequential development of thinking skills or techniques progressing cumulatively up the grade levels. Beyond the obvious fact that as students grow and mature they will think in more sophisticated ways, there is no evidence that the development of thinking fits into some tidy psychological scheme. What matters is that teachers have a clear understanding of what thinking involves and then proceed to teach their students accordingly, testing in their daily work what their students can and cannot do. Thinking is like writing or speaking, it improves with practice, and responds to challenge.

If thinking is to be taught consistently in all subjects and grade levels, four general rules must be followed. First, it must be an active, explicit and deliberate part of any approach to teaching, and it must be demonstrated in the teaching techniques used in the classroom. Second, it must be embedded in students' assignments and activities and, above all, in tests and examinations that so easily fall into a simple memorizing mode. Third, it must be built into reporting systems, so that it is deliberately emphasized on report cards and thus made obvious to students, parents and teachers. Fourth, it must not only be taught in the form of classroom exercises and activities, it must be modelled and demonstrated by teachers.

So far as specific thinking skills are concerned, the research bears out these principles. Frequent, short sessions of skills teaching are more effective than longer ones. Skills are best learned when students are consciously aware of what they are doing. It helps when students are taught to discuss and think about the actual processes of thinking. Skills are best learned when they are seen as serving a useful purpose, rather than as abstract, self-contained exercises. Finally they are best learned when the teacher demonstrates them by her own conduct.

At a more specific level, the literature is full of suggestions for specific techniques for the teaching of particular skills: case-studies, role-playing, dilemmas, problem-solving, and on and on. Among the most interesting techniques are those of Edward de Bono, with his emphasis on the teaching of thinking as a subject in its own right. De Bono has invented a whole series of exercises that students are taught to use in appropriate contexts. They include such labels as PMI (a way of categorizing ideas on a topic as plus, minus, or interesting); OPV (consider other points of view); CAF (consider all factors); and so on. In one sense, such devices seem like gimmicks, but it is precisely this that makes them useful for teaching, enabling students to learn and use them, and in the process to become aware of what it means to think (de Bono:1982). Others urge the value of teaching students an appropriate vocabulary to help them to think more effectively by using and understanding such words as premise, conclusion, hypothesis, generalization, verify, and the rest (Blair:1986).

Above all, whatever is done in teaching must be reflected in the ways in which students' work is evaluated. Assignments, tests and examinations must emphasize thinking. They must provide students with material that they are to analyze and manipulate, for example in the form of cartoons, primary sources, numerical data. In this regard, open-book tests are probably more useful than traditional tests and examinations. Questions must demand a process of reasoning and not simply the recall of the one right answer. They must be marked in ways that make clear that thinking is prized, for example by allocating a certain proportion of marks to the quality of the reasoning and the level of argument used in arriving at an answer.

Finally, so far as context is concerned, it is useful to refer back to what Paul and Siegel have described as critical thinking in the strong sense, by which they mean that it is a disposition to act far more than it is a simple set of academic skills. Thus, students must see that thinking is encouraged and welcomed and that it is one of the key components of school life. For example, teachers should make continuing reference to it. Classroom displays should feature it. School and classroom rules should be consistent with the value of clear thinking. Examples of effective thinkers and thinking must be provided in the context of appropriate subject-matter. Controversial issues must not be avoided in the classroom, since they provide rich material for thinking. Students must feel comfortable and confident in their classrooms so that they are not afraid to voice their opinions. In short, all aspects of school and classroom life should demonstrate the value given to thinking.

None of this should be taken to mean that the teaching of specific thinking techniques or skills is all that is involved in teaching students to think more adequately. There is at the moment considerable enthusiasm in educational circles for the teaching of critical thinking skills, but, while useful, such skills can take us only so far. They are useful, and perhaps even necessary, but certainly not sufficient. There is a dimension to thinking that goes beyond skills. And getting a good mark in Critical Thinking 201 is certainly no indication of any ability to think in real terms about real problems.

A musician, for example, can be a superb technician, reading music at sight, playing notes cleanly, executing flawlessly, following a score to the last detail, without necessarily playing well. There is something in musical performance that goes beyond technique or skill. To take another example, a person can be a skilled bricklayer, but laying bricks does not of itself produce a good house, or even a good wall. Similarly with thinking, using the techniques of constructing or dissecting an argument does not guarantee that the argument will be compelling.

This goes beyond the obvious point that thinking skills, like any other techniques, can be used for unacceptable purposes. The more important point is that thinking skills or techniques are only a part of thinking, not the whole of it. To think means having something to say, even if it is said badly. And having something to say means having knowledge and experience upon which to draw. It involves a capacity for reflection, for the posing of questions.

Thinking cannot be divorced from subject-matter. It cannot be taught as a set of skills isolated from any content. One cannot think in the abstract. One must think about something. Thinking is enriched by knowledge. The more one knows about something, the easier it is to think about it. Thinking is not a matter of playing intellectual word-games. It means engaging in a serious way with important and worthwhile problems.

At the same time, it is going too far to reject any concept of thinking skills. Technical expertise alone will not make for a good musician, but it certainly helps. Though the language of thinking skills is easily overdone, they do have their place. In any thinking worthy of the name, skills are at work. It is useful to know that merely quoting an authority can never prove a point. It is useful to know the rules of elementary logic. At the very least, anyone who does not know such things is likely to be at the mercy of those who do. More important, to know them enables one to think more adequately.

On the practical level, thinking skills can certainly be useful in the classroom. Many good teachers have found useful material in the various critical thinking schemes and approaches that now exist. We have too often assumed that teaching factual knowledge automatically confers an ability to think. But knowing the details of the Congress of Vienna does not in itself tell one anything about the nature of history, or the nature of politics, international relations, or anything else. On its own, it is simply a "bunch of stuff," as my students used to tell me. If anyone objects that the Congress of Vienna is not exactly likely to enthrall students anyway, or that it is somehow irrelevant, the same argument applies to the Winnipeg General Strike, the Oka crisis, or any other socially relevant topic. They all too easily lie lifeless in the textbook. They are nothing more than "inert ideas," to use Whitehead's expressive phrase.The antidote may lie in the importance given to such activities as press-conferences in chemistry projects as proposed by La maîtresse d'école (Maîtress d'école, 1989: 121) and in the famous War Toys project of Pacijou in Québec (Maîtresse d'école, 1989: p.ix; OS/OS, II, 2 (April 1990) 29-41 and OS/OS, II, 3 (September 1990) 17-18).Thinking is more than memorizing, though memorizing can be necessary to thinking. It is a silly but all too common mistake to see them as mutually exclusive. But, if we want students to think, whether in the sense of using some specific technique or skill, or in the sense of reflecting upon and asking questions about some big idea, we must provide them with the opportunity and the example. Thinking does not come easily. It must be taught and learned. As teachers, we must think about thinking.

5. Teachers Must Connect What They Are Teaching To Students' Previous Knowledge And Experience

In many classrooms when students are asked to learn something, they are given little or no explanation as to why or how it matters. Not susprisingly they fail to see any connection with anything that they already know or think they need to know. If students think about it at all, they realize that they are required to learn because the teacher (or the curriculum) says so, or because "it will be on the test." More often, they simply accept it as part of the ritual associated with attending school.

As a result, learning is debased. It is seen as nothing more than the picking up of inert ideas that need to be remembered for only a short time and can then be safely forgotten. Learning is separated from life and school-learning is seen as having little or nothing to do with anything except obtaining grades. In the process, what students do know is either ignored or under-rated. They are led to believe — sometimes quite directly — that what they do know is not important. Thus, school appeals primarily to those who already share its values or who are prepared to do so, those who for one reason or another think that they will get something out of it. Many such students, especially those from middle-class backgrounds, realize from the example of their parents that school is an important step towards getting a good job. Some realize that school has at least the potential to open up a new world and so are prepared to cooperate with it in order to see what this new world has to offer. Other students, however, see little point in learning what they are expected to learn and, as a result, see little point in school. Unable to see any connection between school-learning and their own lives, they reject the former in order to concentrate on the latter. Many such students are from the working class, for whom the standard academic curriculum has little intrinsic appeal. Thus, as I've indicated, demands have arisen for the creation of a specifically working-class curriculum that would be more culturally relevant to most students' experience.

The obvious risks of ghettoization through a working-class curriculum, as mentioned above, mean that it is not necessarily the best way to make school attractive to those students who do not automatically accept it. If the standard curriculum has little inherent appeal for many students, this does not automatically mean that the curriculum must be scrapped. It is the task of pedagogy to bridge the gap between students and the curriculum, to make it accessible and interesting to them and to show them why it is worth learning. This, of course, assumes that it is in fact worth learning. It should go without saying that one of the important tasks of teachers is not to manipulate students into an unquestioning faith that the curriculum will be good for them, but rather to teach them to approach it critically.

In practical terms, teachers have a duty to connect what they want students to learn with their existing knowledge and experience. It is not acceptable to treat the curriculum as a given and then to find some way to push it into students, whether by force or by charm. It must be organized, and reorganized (and, where necessary, abandoned) so that they find it accessible, worthwhile, and even interesting.

Don Sawyer nicely describes this task of reorganizing the curriculum in his account of his teaching in Newfoundland. He was teaching a Grade 10 class about ancient Mesopotamia without much success, when one of his students asked, "Aren't they fighting over there now?" "Yeah, they sure are," answered Sawyer, and, when someone asked why, he began with religion, only to find that the students knew very little about the region. In Sawyer's words, "In a class of twenty grade ten students, not one knew the primary religion of Israel, much less of the surrounding countries. We had been spending a month and a half on the political shifts of ancient Mesopotamia while one of the major trouble spots of the world was a total mystery." At that point, Sawyer decided to talk matters over with his students — a sensible decision but one that many teachers are surprisingly reluctant to take. One thing the students quickly agreed on: they were all fed up with their textbook. One girl voiced the wish that they could throw it away. Sawyer said they could if they could find a better way to use the time. When they were not convinced, he threw it out the window: a dramatic way of demystifying the curriculum and opening it up to challenge! He went on to explain, however, that the textbook need not be automatically rejected, and that it could be put to use if approached differently. From this basis, Sawyer reorganized the curriculum:

> The final form of our history class did not take shape for several more weeks, but for the time being I began to record the CBC local and national news twice a week. Since virtually none of the kids listened to the news or (since none were available) read newspapers, I played the recording in class and we discussed the main points. This was the start of a process that turned our history class into a study of the social realities of the world, the country, the community and perhaps most significantly the school, and how these realities affected our lives. (Sawyer, 1979:61-63)

The episode reveals a teacher faced with the common problem of having to teach a body of knowledge to students who found no meaning in it. In this case, Sawyer took the curriculum, looked for a point of connection with his students, reworked the subject matter by putting it in the context of current affairs as presented on the news, and opened it up to students for analysis and discussion. What would otherwise have been static and disconnected information was brought to life by recasting it in a way that connected it with students' knowledge and experience.

Sylvia Ashton-Warner took a similar approach when teaching reading and writing to Maori children in New Zealand. She quickly rejected the official texts, with their Dick and Jane characters, that had no message for her students except to tell them that they were different from the alleged norm. Instead, Ashton-Warner decided to organize her reading and writing lessons around "key-words" that the children themselves provided and that arose from their experience. As she describes the approach:

> Back to first words. To these first books. They must be made out of the stuff of the child itself. I reach a hand into the mind of the child, bring out a handful of the stuff I find there, and use that as our first working material. Whether it is good or bad stuff, violent or placid stuff, coloured or dun. To effect an unbroken beginning. And in this dynamic material, within the familiarity and security of it, the Maori finds that words have intense meaning to him (*sic*), from which cannot help but arise a love of reading. (Ashton-Warner, 1963:34)

As one thinks about the implications of both examples — of Sawyer and Ashton-Warner — it quickly becomes clear that a certain tension is involved in connecting curriculum to students' knowledge and experience. The problem can be simply expressed: How far are teachers entitled to go in reorganizing curriculum to provide some point of contact with students? Or, to put it another way, which comes first: the curriculum or the students?

Pedagogical theory provides two answers. One insists that students come first and the curriculum second. In this view, an acceptable curriculum (acceptable philosophically, politically, ethically and psychologically) must flow from students' experience and concerns. No curriculum is acceptable if it is designed externally to any particular group of students. The other answer is more cautious: it acknowledges the existence of an external curriculum, and indeed accepts its desirability, but sees a crucial task for pedagogy in making the curriculum meaningful to students. In this view, students and curriculum are not ranked as first and second, but as co-equal. It is, of course, possible to put the curriculum first and the students second (here it is, now learn it), as indeed is the case in many classrooms, but this is not the position that is being advanced here.

In practice, it is not always easy to keep these two answers separate. Most of those who argue that any worthwhile curriculum can be built only upon students' concerns and experience accept that it must also include much of the information that would be found in the standard curriculum. John Dewey, for example, argued that conventional subject matter is a fundamentally important component of education, but he was convinced that it was ineffective and undesirable to begin with conventional subjects, since students were neither able nor ready to understand them. Nonetheless, even for Dewey, the knowledge contained in conventional subject-matter represents, if not the beginning point, the destination of education: "When education is based in theory and practice upon experience, it goes without saying that the organized subject-matter of the adult and the specialist cannot provide the starting point. Nonetheless, it represents the goal toward which education should continuously move" (Dewey, 1938:83).

A contemporary expression of this viewpoint, though not identical in every respect, can be found in the work of Henry Giroux. In Giroux's view, critical pedagogy "... takes the problems and needs of the students themselves as its starting point." This seems clear enough, though it rather understates the difficulty of defining those problems and needs, and of deciding whether they are best met by the school or by some other agency. At the same time, according to Giroux, student experience must be treated as "... an object of inquiry rather than an unproblematic given." As they stand, these words suggest that students' problems and needs are to be treated not so much as things to be solved and met, but as objects of inquiry and analysis, which seems a particularly cold and clinical approach. It is difficult to see why we should begin with students' problems and needs, if we are to treat them only as objects of inquiry. In addition, critical pedagogy "... attempts to provide students with the critical knowledge and skills necessary for them to examine their own particular lived experiences and cultural resources." Such knowledge will presumably be drawn from such fields as history, literature, sociology and so on, so that students will be introduced to more or less conventional subject-matter, though not necessarily in conventional ways. The object, says Giroux, is not to please students but to empower them, and student experience as such must therefore be neither endorsed nor rejected. Rather, teachers must "... create an affirmative and critical continuity between how students view the world and those forms of analyses that provide the basis for both analyzing and enriching such perspectives." Giroux concludes that:

> ... at the heart of any critical pedagogy is the necessity for teachers to work with the knowledge that students actually have. Although this may seem risky and in some cases dangerous, it provides the basis for validating the ways in which students see the world as well as giving them the intellectual content for putting knowledge and meaning into their own categories of meaning and cultural capital. (Giroux, 1988:197-8)

There are some problems with this, not least in the idea that we should necessarily validate the way in which students see the world (for they might well see the world in very limited, partial and unacceptable ways), but overall it seems that we have ended up in a position that is not so very different from that associated with the classical notion of liberal education. We may indeed begin with students' experience, problems and needs, but along the way we should introduce them to a wide range of knowledge, so that they can think about their experience, problems and needs in richer and more comprehensive ways.

Whether to move from students' experience to the curriculum or whether to begin with the curriculum and find a way to link it to students' experience, is a decision that will depend on a specific context. I once knew a student-teacher, for example, who asked me how to make Manitoba history interesting to a Grade 7 class. After watching the class, I told him that it could not be done, that his problem lay in having to teach that particular subject to those particular students. My advice was that he follow Sawyer's example, discuss it with his students, look for ways to use Manitoba history as a source with which to approach more contemporary topics that would make some connection with students, and, in this particular case, think in terms not solely of teaching history, but of teaching it to a particular group of students. Similarly, early in my own teaching career, I was assigned to teach a collection of short stories to an unruly group of twelve-year-olds. The stories dated from the early 1900's and were typical adventure stories of that era. Once I read them, I found them objectionable because of their racism, sexism and imperialism (this occurred in 1960; I doubt that such stories would be used in schools today). However, politics aside, my immediate problem was that my students made their dislike very apparent and my life very miserable. My solution was obvious, and I very quickly found some alternative stories that the students seemed to find more acceptable. I could still pursue the approved objectives (grammar, creative writing, discussion skills, and the rest), though with a different selection of subject-matter. In both cases, the only useful approach to take was to begin with the students and shape the curriculum accordingly. In other cases, with more amenable students, it might have been equally possible to work with the curriculum more or less at it stood — provided, of course, that it was ethically and philosophically acceptable.

There are, in any case, obvious practical limits within which most teachers must work. It is a fact of life for anyone working within the public school system that there is a provincial curriculum, and that increasingly it is backed up by province-wide tests or examinations, with teachers coming under increasing pressure to stick closely to it. Moreover, it is not easy to see how a teacher could work with a curriculum deriving from students' needs, concerns and experience, in a class consisting of thirty or so students, as is the case in most schools. Finally, any curriculum based upon a concept of citizenship must contain that body of knowledge that is judged necessary for the formation of citizenship: it cannot be left somehow to emerge from the experience and concerns of students. So we are left with the pedagogical problem of how to connect the curriculum that exists with the students who are expected to learn from it.

It bears repeating that this does not mean that teachers should simply accept the curriculum unchallenged. Any curriculum is open to question and students must be taught to question it. Why is this topic included? Why is this excluded? Whose interests are being served, and whose are not? Why is the curriculum organized this way rather than another? Indeed, we would be doing students a considerable service simply by taking them through the curriculum. For the vast majority of students, learning is governed by their textbooks and by their teachers' instructions and directions. They rarely if ever see the curriculum that they are required to study. Beyond this first basic step, teachers should, where necessary, feel free to reshape the curriculum, or to depart from it, where it is demonstrably not working in the interests of their students.

With all this understood, however, there still remains the challenge of connecting the curriculum to the knowledge and experience of students. There are, in essence, three ways to do this. First, the teacher presents the material to be learned in terms that students are familiar with and can understand. Second, the teacher draws on knowledge that the students already have and uses this as a base for new learning. Third, the teacher creates experiences that act as springboards for students' learning. None of these three approaches is particularly complicated, but each could benefit from a brief explanation.

The first is something that most teachers do as a matter of routine, turning the x's and y's of algebra problems into apples and oranges, or comparing a character in history to someone known to students. I once watched a student-teacher introducing the idea of regionalism to a class of Grade 9 students by organizing them into groups according to the part of the room in which they were sitting, and getting each group to inventory its resources. Some groups had more space than others, one controlled the windows, another owned the classroom library, one privileged group controlled the doorway, the light switches and the thermostat, another less fortunate group sat in the middle of the room and owned nothing at all of importance. From this beginning, the students were led into an examination of the pro's and con's of cooperating and competing, and the whole experience led into an examination of regional politics in Canada.

This example also serves to illustrate the second approach, in which the teacher draws on knowledge the students already have. This approach can also be seen at work in the example of the Industrial Revolution described earlier. Here the teacher selected something with which students were familiar — the idea of time and its impact on our lives — and used it as a way into the otherwise fairly remote history of the Industrial Revolution. A similar approach was at work in the example of teaching about the Greek city-state through the idea of community.

The third approach works along similar lines except that, rather than relying only on what students already know, the teacher creates an experience that sets the scene for learning. This can be done through simulation and role-playing, for example, as well as through the use of dilemmas in which students are asked what they would do (or what they think a particular character would do) in a certain situation. In science, experiments and demonstrations can be organized in which the results run contrary to students' predictions, thus creating a problem that needs to be resolved. Bruner's use of sentence structure, described earlier, provides another example of this type of creation of experience.

However it is done, it is important that teachers do everything they can to connect the curriculum with student's knowledge and experiences. We best learn new or unfamiliar material by linking it with what we already know. In doing so, we also extend, enrich and revise what we already know. In Piaget's terms, we do not simply assimilate new material, we also accommodate (i.e., revise, shape, rethink) what we already know so that it fits with what we are learning. In this way, to use Dewey's term, education becomes the reconstruction of experience. This also does students the courtesy of treating their knowledge seriously and therefore shows them that they know more than they themselves often realize. They do not stand in front of the curriculum ignorant and empty, but as makers of meaning, active learners and thinkers.

6. Students Must Become Active In Their Own Learning

There is, of course, nothing new in this recommendation. As far back as Plato, one can find arguments that children learn best through play and activity, and it has been a common theme of educational writers and theorists for about two thousand years. Modern psychology has given it a further boost with its insistence that effective teaching must take into account the ways in which children learn and, since at a certain stage in their development they learn best through activity, teaching must promote activity-based learning.

Despite such exhortations, teaching has often followed a different course, relying primarily on shoving information into students. There are various reasons for this, but a large part of the explanation must be sought in the theory of learning that for many years dominated pedagogical thought and action, and that continues to be influential. In simple terms, this was a theory grounded in the concept of stimulus and response. Like an experimental psychologist working with rats or pigeons, teachers presented a stimulus and worked with their students until they produced the appropriate response. For example, when the teacher said "2 x 2," students were trained to say "4." Whether they understood the operations involved was not the point; what mattered was that they could perform them. Those of us old enough to remember will recall this kind of thing at work in the various spelling drills, mental arithmetic exercises, and recitations that occupied our school days. The key word was "drill," with all its revealing suggestions of military training in which novice soldiers repeat an exercise endlessly until it becomes second nature to them.

This approach should not be rejected out of hand. There are, obviously, many occasions in life when it is useful to be able to recall a bit of knowledge with little or no thought. For example, life becomes both simpler and more controlled when we can spell and calculate automatically.

However, while it has its uses, the approach came to dominate almost all aspects of education, at least at the school level. Geography became a matter of capes and bays, a catalogue of terms and place-names. History became little more than a list of names, events and dates. Learning a second language meant memorizing vocabulary, grammar and a few stock phrases but without being able to speak it. Science became not a matter of doing and thinking about experiments, but of mastering formulas and equations. As one Canadian scientist recently put it: "... we can't deal with the kids in a way we can challenge them. The real problem is we can't really show them that science isn't just a collection of facts. Science is a way of thinking. Science is a process.... We teach them all the facts, but never give them a chance to participate. They never catch the thrill or the excitement of the game" (Zoologist Dr. David Ogilvie of the University of Western Ontario, quoted in *The Globe and Mail*, September 8, 1990, p.D4.). In short, much pedagogy came to be dominated by stimulus-response theory, reinforced by compulsory examinations that emphasized the remembering of factual information. In the process, to learn meant little more than to memorize and repeat. It had little or nothing to do with understanding and applying knowledge.

In recent years, an alternative view of learning has emerged, associated particularly with cognitive psychology. Stimulus-response theory is behaviourist in its orientation. It is concerned above all with how people behave, with what they actually do, and not with their reasons and motives, their internal states of mind. As has often been said, the learner is seen as a black box. A stimulus goes in and a response emerges; how the stimulus is translated into the response, what goes on in the learner's mind, is not a concern.

By contrast, cognitive psychology stresses the activity of the learner, who is seen as a maker of meaning. Instead of responding more or less automatically to a stimulus, the learner is seen as someone who does not merely receive a stimulus but as someone who shapes it. Years ago, Piaget anticipated this view when he said that learning consists of two processes: assimilation and accommodation. We assimilate a new experience or new information by incorporating it into what we already know, but at the same time we accommodate or reshape what we already know to fit with the new experience or information. These two processes work together, sometimes in harmony and sometimes in conflict. It is this conflict, or disequilibrium, that produces learning, since it causes us actively to make sense out of our experience. For Piaget, learning is an active process in which the learner seeks to make sense out of or to reconstruct experience. As he put it, anything is learned only to the extent that it is reinvented.

This is a key theme in cognitive psychology, which sees learning as an active process: not the reception of stimuli but the creation of meaning, and thus intimately connected with such things as inquiry, creativity and critical thinking. Its implications for pedagogy are quickly apparent. Teachers still have to provide a stimulus (a demonstration, an explanation, a question and so on). and students still have to provide a response, but we are now learning to pay much more attention to what happens when the stimulus is converted into a response. One application of this is to be seen in mathematics teachers' belief that the actual answer to a problem (right or wrong) is no more important than the process by which their students arrive at it.

However, though it is important that students can provide correct answers — at least to those problems that have answers that are unequivocally right or wrong — correctness is only a part of learning. The behaviourist approach, strictly applied, concerns itself only with ensuring that students provide the correct answer. Cognitive psychology embraces a wider range of concerns, prompting teachers to consider such questions as: What were students thinking when they worked on the problem? Can they justify their answer? Can they compare it with similar questions? Can they apply it in a new setting? Indeed, cognitive psychology suggests that teaching deliberately involve students in discussing such questions, so that they become aware of their own thought-processes and learn to think about their own thinking.

What it all means is that students must be active in their own learning, and teachers must acknowledge them as active makers of meaning. Active learning does not necessarily mean hands-on learning, involving the manipulation of concrete objects or lots of physical movement in the classroom, or students busily working in groups, and so on. Active learning is more than activity-based learning. There are, for example, such things as active listening and active observation. If students are listening to a well-told story, or watching an absorbing film, they are likely to be physically still and quiet, but it would be absurd to say they are not learning. Their bodies may be still, but their minds will be working vigorously. Verbal learning can be meaningful. The key points are that students must be actively involved in their own learning, and that this active involvement can take many forms, among them listening, reading, watching, experimenting, questioning, communicating, brainstorming, discussing and reporting. The list could go on and on, but the point is a simple one. Active learning means that students must think about and be involved with what they are learning, and they can do this in many different ways.

All the examples of teaching described in this book illustrate these points. In all of them, students were engaged in, contributing to and thinking about what they were learning, and in doing so, also thinking about what they were learning, and what they already knew. Piaget's two processes of assimilation and accommodation were both in operation.

At the same time, in all the examples, worthwhile learning was taking place. Neither activity nor active learning is its own justification. Activity must be educationally worthwhile. Those of us who have been through military training, for example, were all taught to use the bayonet. We learned how to charge, how to thrust and twist the bayonet, how to use our foot to hold down our victim while we pulled the bayonet out, how to scream to keep up our courage and intimidate the enemy. It was a very active form of learning: we charged, we lunged, we practised and we screamed. Whether it was a worthwhile form of learning (at least in the educational sense) is open to question. To take a less stark example, I am always struck by the way in which younger students are often directed to draw a title page when beginning a new unit of study in social studies. I have seen students spending two or three periods designing, drawing, colouring and doing whatever they felt necessary to prepare a decorative title page. If they were learning something about art it might not be so bad, but, in the vast majority of instances, the students are simply using time that could be better spent, especially in social studies, in considering issues of substance. They would use their time better in discussing Socrates, or the position of women, or the nature of citizenship in the city-state, than using it to prepare a colourful title page on Ancient Greece.

Worthwhileness is, however, a slippery concept. Like beauty, it is in the eye of the beholder. Anarchists, Marxists, socialists, liberals, conservatives, nationalists, feminists, environmentalists — all have their own view of what is worthwhile in education.

Dewey argued that the only acceptable test to apply to an educational activity was to ask the question: does it enhance growth? In other words, does it empower students, does it enable them to achieve their potential, does it maximize their choices both now and for the future? As the nineteenth century socialist, William Morris put it, education must enable people to make the most of their talents in all directions. Perhaps the most pedagogically useful examination of what worthwhileness means has been provided by James Raths:

All other things being equal, one activity is more worthwhile than another:

1. If it permits children to make informed choices in carrying out the activity and to reflect on the consequences of their choices.

2. If it assigns to students active roles in the learning situation rather than passive ones.

3. If it asks students to engage in inquiry into ideas, application of intellectual processes, or current problems, either personal or social.

4. If it involves children with reality (i.e., real objects, materials and artifacts).

5. If completion of the activity may be accomplished successfully by children at several different levels of ability.

6. If it asks students to examine in a new setting an idea, an application of an intellectual process, or a current problem which has been previously studied.

7. If it requires students to examine topics or issues that citizens in our society do not normally examine — and that are typically ignored by the major communication media in the nation.

8. If it involves students and faculty members in 'risk' taking — not a risk of life or limb, but a risk of success or failure.

9. If it requires students to rewrite, rehearse, and polish their initial efforts.

10. If it involves students in the application and mastery of rules, standards, or disciplines.

11. If it gives students a chance to share the planning, the carrying out of a plan, or the results of an activity with others.

12. If it is relevant to the expressed purposes of the students (Raths, 1971).

This list of criteria does more than provide an extremely helpful check-list for deciding whether teaching is worthwhile or not in any particular instance. It also incorporates the concept of active learning that has been described in these pages. It should be central to the thinking of anyone concerned with pedagogy, whether theoretically or practically.

One final point is worth making, especially in view of the connection between pedagogy and citizenship upon which this book is based. It is this: it seems perfectly reasonable to assume that students who are encouraged to be active in their own learning will carry with them in their lives outside and after school a set of attitudes and dispositions that will assist them in being active citizens. They will have become accustomed to think, to ask questions, to establish a personal connection with what they have to undertake, and so they are unlikely to be passive or apathetic in their social and political lives. Active learning serves to empower students. Stimulus and response teaching leaves students powerless before the curriculum and the teacher. Like Pavlov's dogs salivating at the sound of a bell, their task is simply to provide an appropriate response upon demand. Active learning, on the other hand, which treats students as creators of meaning, serves to develop instead of frustrate the talents and abilities of students. The result is the emergence of a sense of efficacy and empowerment that both enhances the quality of citizenship and works to prevent the creation of the unacceptable distinction between those who succeed and those who fail.

That there is a strong link between active learning and active citizenship is suggested most clearly by European educational practice. My own English schooling may serve as a convenient example. At age eleven, having passed various tests, I was selected to attend a "grammar school," the first step towards a career of upward mobility. Most of my friends on the street where I lived were not so selected and so went to "secondary modern schools." There they received a vocationally-oriented program aimed at turning them out into the work force at fifteen. I got an academically-oriented program aimed at grooming me for university or the professions. I was, in effect, being educated out of the working class. Having grown up with a fairly clear picture of a world divided into "them" and "us," I was to be induted into the ranks of "them." Dress, grooming, speech, deportment, knowledge — all were to be shaped. However, though we were given a high-powered academic curriculum (French, Latin, English, history, mathematics and the rest), the teaching was quite routine — until we reached the age of sixteen. Those of us who then stayed at school suddenly found ourselves in a different pedagogical world altogether. Classes became much smaller; teachers became more egalitarian; seminar and discussion became the rule; rather than learning masses of facts, we were now led to explore problems; we were exempted from most school rules; in a wide variety of ways it was made clear to us that we were being inducted into a new world, one more like a gentleman's club than a school (at the age of eleven, the sexes were separated.) Above all, active learning was encouraged. We were being trained to be leaders not followers; givers not takers of orders; and the pedagogy served to make this plain. It delivered a clear message: mass schooling was good enough for the masses, but for us, the fortunate few, a different form of teaching was provided. Since we were to be the truly active citizens, the leaders of the future, the bearers of civilization, our teachers had to teach us to be active learners.

This is, admittedly, an English example and goes back more than forty years, but though school structures have changed, the underlying pattern remains the same. The higher students are up the social ladder and the more likely they are to occupy positions of power in later life, the more likely they are to experience a pedagogy that promotes active learning. Conversely, the lower students are on the social ladder, the more likely they are to meet a pedagogy that does not move beyond stimulus and response.

Active learning, then, is more than a pedagogical tool. Like so much else in pedagogy, it also serves a political purpose.

7. Students Should Share And Build Upon Each Other's Ideas

When we picture students' learning, especially in a school setting, we often imagine them sitting at their desks, hunched over a book or some paper, brow furrowed, eyes tightened in concentration, pen or pencil in hand. In this picture, learning is a solitary, individual business. It consists of whatever is going on in one's head while listening to someone else, or reading a book, or solving a problem. Historically, schools emphasized this kind of learning. They frowned upon students working together, labelled sharing as cheating, and insisted that students must do their own work. At the same time, they made this style of learning not only solitary but also competitive, as children were encouraged to compete to be first with the right answer, to do better than anyone else on a test, to outshine their classmates. Many students were caught up in this view of learning as a struggle for superiority, and eagerly took up the spirit of competition. Others resisted and in some cases established their own counter-culture in which cooperating with the teacher and playing the academic game were decidedly frowned upon. In this atmosphere, students who received A's and other such marks of teacher favour were rejected as sucks, swots, ear-'oles, and teacher's pets.

Over the years we have increasingly come to realize that any view of learning that sees it as solitary and individualistic — the lonely student frowning over her or his paper — is incomplete. It mistakes what is only one kind of learning for learning as a whole. Obviously, there is a place for solitary learning. There are times when we all have to withdraw into isolation in order to concentrate upon a particular task. Learning some vocabulary, solving a mathematics problem, practising a sports skill, writing an essay, thinking through a problem in a relationship — these and many other things usually require a period of quiet time for thought and reflection. At the same time, there comes a point when we need the help and advice of other people. Having learned our vocabulary, we need someone to quiz us or to hear us say our new words. Having thought through a problem in a relationship, we need to bounce our ideas off someone else, to get a second and third opinion. In short, there is an obvious social side to learning: it is not all a matter of finding some privacy and "hitting the books." We need to hear other people's ideas, to learn from their experience, to respond to their questions and suggestions. We learn not only from solitary study, but from conversation and discussion, from the mutual sharing and questioning of ideas and information. Until fairly recently, it seemed that this was recognized everywhere but in the school, where students were enjoined to work in silence, to stay at their own desks, to do no more and no less than what they were told. John Dewey once wrote of his experience in looking for work-tables for his elementary school and of being unable to find what he wanted. Store after store could offer him only individual desks (and some of us can remember the days when they were bolted to the floor), until finally one salesperson identified the problem: "... I am afraid we have not what you want. You want something at which the children may work. These are all for listening!" (Dewey, 1915:31). Such days are now in the past, and schools have tables, work-stations and learning centres, which make it possible for students to work together. All the examples of teaching described in this book show students working together as well as with their teachers. All the lessons described provided opportunity for students to voice opinions, to offer suggestions and ideas, to ask questions and raise arguments.

The common experience is that when this is done, the quality of learning markedly improves. It does so for two broad reasons. First, the level of information, of argument and of ideas, is raised. When up to thirty students (or even more these days) whether in groups or as a whole class, are thinking about a topic that they see as important or interesting, there is almost no limit to what is brought into the discussion. In this age of instant information and universal communication, even the most unlikely students often prove to possess surprising knowledge, gleaned from some television quiz show or chance experience. Second, in such an atmosphere, students learn that their own ideas are more interesting than they might have realized. Instead of being "dumbed-out", to use Bob Davis's expressive phrase, and seeing themselves as stupid or uninformed, they develop confidence in their powers. They become more alert, more motivated and more empowered. And since nothing succeeds like success, they become increasingly so. At the same time, they learn that ideas, information and questions, can come from anyone. The traditional classroom division between the slow and the smart begins to break down, as even the apparently slowest student proves to have something useful and intelligent to say. Douglas Barnes has revealing examples of this process at work in a science class in *From Communication to Curriculum* (37-47 and 94-96).

All this makes not only for worthwhile learning, it also provides valuable lessons in democratic citizenship as the classroom becomes more collegial, more sharing and more participatory. School ceases to be the process whereby some make it and others do not, where students learn that they will become either makers or takers of orders, either leaders or followers. Instead, it becomes the place where students learn that everyone has ability, that everyone has an important contribution to make to the common good, not simply as a hewer of wood or a drawer of water, but as an active and critical participant in the continuing debate that is at the heart of any society.

It is not difficult to see how this approach to learning would work out in classroom practice. The basic steps are these:

First, the teacher must establish a classroom environment in which the students feel a sense of ownership and belonging, and in which they feel free to offer their opinions, secure in the knowledge that they will be taken seriously.

Second, the students must possess the necessary skills and attitudes to make social learning work. They do not automatically develop the ability to participate in democratic discussion. Left to themselves, they are very likely to hog the spotlight, to shout down their classmates, to see what they want to say as more important, more urgent, and more interesting than anything else. Social learning, then, must be taught, and the techniques of cooperative learning can be very useful in this regard.

Third, the teacher must organize the material to be taught as issues or problems to be investigated instead of simply as facts to be learned. Obviously, facts and information are important. It is too easy for discussion to degenerate into an ignorant exchange of prejudice and ignorance in which no-one learns anything, except that they are right and everyone else is irredeemably wrong. But facts become more interesting, and are more effectively learned, when they are considered in the context of examining or exploring a problem. I have already examined this problem-posing approach to teaching, but it might be useful to say something more about the first two points, dealing with the establishment of an appropriate classroom environment and with ensuring that students have the necessary skills and attitudes.

It seems that some teacher traits are better than others when it comes to establishing a good classroom environment. Teachers have been described, for instance, as either dominative or integrative. The former type works against students and is very much concerned with personal power and status. The dominative teacher issues orders, controls ideas, uses threat and blame and avoids exchange of opinions with students. In contrast, the integrative teacher works with students, uses requests and suggestions rather than orders, consults students and encourages the exchange of ideas. The evidence is — and one thinks of the work of Sarah Lightfoot described earlier — that students' behaviour changes according to the teacher's style.

There is some similarity here with the work of Carl Rogers, who has suggested that teachers who work best with students all possess certain traits. They are "real" and do not hide behind any kind of teacher mask. They value and trust their students and empathize with them. They work on the assumption that students want to learn, and learn best when they see what they are learning as relevant to their own goals (Rogers, 1969).

Dominative teachers enforce a status different from that of their integrative colleagues. Integrative teachers assume a status that, while acknowledging the power and authority vested in their role, nonetheless does not dominate students. They exercise their responsibility to direct and guide students, but in ways that take seriously students' ideas and experience. They are neither authoritarian nor permissive, but adopt a status that gives students room to exercise their own power in educationally worthwhile ways.

Teachers should also have a wide range of skills at their disposal. Flanders, for example, has argued that the skills of what he calls "indirect" teaching produce a more positive classroom climate than does "direct" teaching. Specifically, these skills include accepting, clarifying and supporting students' ideas and feelings; praising and encouraging; and asking questions to encourage participation and to solicit ideas. Conversely, direct teaching includes lecturing, giving orders, criticizing, and justifying one's own authority. Other skills that improve a classroom environment include the ability to build teaching upon problems that students see as worthwhile; to provide for student participation; to cater to different styles of learning; and to provide a wide range of student resources. The list could go on and on, but the point is clear: there are skills that teachers can learn and apply that can influence classroom climate. In this regard, Steven Bossert's work is of interest. He has noted that different teaching strategies produce their own imperatives, forcing teachers to act and students to react in certain ways. For example, teaching a whole class together *via* recitation or some such technique makes it difficult to provide individual assistance to students, since it is awkward to hold up the whole class for one student. Further, in such whole-class approaches, high achievers dominate teachers' attention, since they are usually able to answer the questions, volunteer information and so on. Again, teaching a whole class means that teachers have to provide a uniform, publicly visible system of authority; when misbehaviour occurs, it has to be corrected in view of the whole class and this makes it difficult to apply any personal touch. In addition, it means that students cannot have their misbehaviour explained or discussed, since the whole class could be held up. Thus, the teacher becomes the impersonal enforcer of universal rules, rather than the more personal explainer of misconduct. Furthermore, the teaching of a whole class together makes it impossible for teachers to become involved in activity as participants with their pupils. By contrast, a classroom organization that allows for students to work on a variety of tasks at different levels makes it possible for teachers to work with students in a much more personal way. The point of Bossert's argument is not to show that one approach is better than another, but that different teaching strategies produce different effects, including effects on teacher-student relationships that are so important in establishing classroom climate: "... the task organization of these classrooms influenced the method of control and the extent of teacher involvement in task activities, which in turn affected the development of empathic relationships" (Bossert, 1979:97-8).

Teachers, then, play an important part in establishing classroom environment. So, of course, do students. They have their own agenda, their own definition of the situation. Their attitudes to each other, to school, to the subject they are studying and to their teacher, all affect what happens in the classroom. Over the years, students build up their definition of what teaching is, and this is not something that can be quickly overcome. If, for example, students have come to define teachers as people who give notes and who lecture a great deal, they will not adjust quickly to someone who wants them to begin role-playing. To no-one's surprise, there are no magic solutions to the problems of leading such students to redefine their expectations. There are, however, some goals to work towards. First, a more positive climate will exist to the extent that students feel they have some voice in what is happening in the class. To put it another way, leadership is best when it comes from the group and not just from the teacher. Secondly, students need to feel they are accepted by each other and by their teacher. Third, there should be a reasonably broad definition of what is acceptable behaviour, so that there is not a constant niggling about unnecessary rules. Fourth, there should be a reasonable amount of communication among students.One example of this process at work may be seen in the school co-op meetings and the Wall Journal used in Freinet pedagogy (Freinet, 1990, 87-99).

Beyond this, it will usually be necessary to train students in the skills and attitudes they will need if they are to share and build upon each other's ideas. Much of this will, of course, develop from the pattern of everyday interaction that the teacher establishes in the classroom. The spirit of mutual respect and trust that must exist among students is the result, not of specific rules and injunctions, but of the expectations and patterns of behaviour that the teacher encourages, by example and demonstration, by explanation and persuasion, and, when absolutely necessary, by outright prohibition.

Within this overall context, there are some specific skills that students will need but that are not often explicitly taught, and they concern the carrying out of effective discussion. The approach to teaching and learning taken throughout this book depends for its success upon the use of effective discussion in the classroom, but this is not something that can be taken for granted. As with essay-writing, laboratory experiments, problem-solving or any other skill, successful discussion demands the application of a set of specific skills and should be taught.

One of the most useful attempts to do this is Fawcett Hill's formulation of the Group Cognitive Map. Here, a discussion

group, having done some assigned reading, wo
through nine steps:

1. Definition of terms and concepts.
2. General statement of author's message.
3. Identification of major themes and sub-topics.
4. Allocation of time for discussion of different topics.
5. Discussion of topics and sub-topics.
6. Integration of material with other knowledge.
7. Application of the material.
8. Evaluation of author's arguments.
9. Evaluation of group and individual performance (Fawcett Hill, 1962).

These nine steps are taught and applied systematically until they become almost second nature. They can also be modified to suit one's particular purposes. For example, a less elaborate version is:

1. Summary (in one's own words) of the author's message.
2. Identification of major topics and sub-topics.
3. Discussion of topics and sub-topics.
4. Integration of the material with existing knowledge.
5. Application of the material.
6. Evaluation of the author's message.

As a group becomes familiar with this approach, it becomes less necessary to worry about each specific step. Experienced groups can often telescope steps, interchange them, and generally treat the whole process with flexibility. No matter what, one point is crucial: initially, the steps must be very deliberately taught and applied.

Discussion skills are, of course, only skills, no more and no less. Whether students use them to good effect will depend in large part on the extent to which they are committed to what they are learning and the extent to which they share a common purpose with their teachers and their fellow students. Such a common purpose, moreover, is essential if learning is to be more than a solitary activity. If we fail to see learning as a social activity, we restrict it, and thereby make it less effective both for its own sake and as a vehicle of active, critical citizenship. For too many students, school is not a place where they explore, develop and reveal their talents and demonstrate what they can do, but a place where they are told what they cannot do. They grow into a state of what some psychologists have called "learned helplessness," afraid or unwilling to exert their independence and convinced that school has nothing to offer them.

Working from British experience, David Hargreaves has written that for many working-class students, school has caused "... a destruction of their dignity which is so massive and pervasive that few subsequently recover from it" (Hargreaves, 1982:61). He links this with what he calls the overly academic nature of the curriculum: "... the very concept of ability becomes closely tied to the intellectual-cognitive. Intelligence becomes defined as the ability to master the cognitive-intellectual aspects of school subjects" (Hargreaves, 1982:17). The problem with this argument, however, is that for many students, and especially for those who are labelled as "non-academic," there is little that is "cognitive-intellectual" in what they are required to do in school. They are overwhelmingly required to fill in worksheets, follow instructions, and complete a variety of low-level tasks, all designed on the assumption that, since there is not much that they can do, they must be given tasks that will allow them a taste of success. Alternatively, as in Sawyer's Newfoundland outport school, they will be routinely failed. Sawyer's solution, like that of any good teacher, was not to abandon intellectual work and academic subject matter, but to find new ways of approaching them that combined much of the traditional content with students' experience and skills. An integral part of his approach, as in all good teaching, was to encourage, and indeed to require, students to share and build upon each other's ideas and insights.

8. Connections Must Be Established Between The Classroom And The World Outside The School

In H.G. Wells' 1910 novel, *The New Machiavelli*, the central character, Remington, thinks back to his school days in London:

> Here all about me was London, a vast inexplicable being, a vortex of gigantic forces, that filled and overwhelmed me with impressions, and stirred my imagination to a perpetual vague inquiry; and my school not only offered no key to it, but had practically no comment to make upon it at all. We were within three miles of Westminster and Charing Cross, the government offices of a fifth of mankind (*sic*) were all within an hour's stroll, great economic changes were going on under our eyes, now the hoardings flamed with election placards, now the Salvation Army and now the unemployed came trailing in procession through the winter grey streets, now the newspaper placards outside news-shops told of battles in strange places, now of amazing discoveries, now of sinister crimes, abject squalor and poverty, imperial splendour and luxury. . . . We went across St. Margaret's Close and through the school gate into a quiet puerile world apart from all these things. We joined in the earnest acquirement of all that was necessary for Greek epigrams and Latin verses, and for the rest played games. (Wells, 1910:59-60)

In Wells' words, it was a "... submerged and isolated curriculum" that "... did not even join on to living interests where it might have done so" (Wells, 1910:63). Such isolation is no longer as common as it was, and schools have increasingly made at least some point of contact with the world outside their walls. Speakers visit the classroom; students go on field trips; the media bring the world into the school; curricula explicitly address current events and issues. Life and learning, school and society, are no longer separated as much as they once were.

They must, indeed, never be separated and teachers must always make sure that their teaching makes a connection between the classroom and the outside world. We have long known that effective pedagogy means establishing a link between what students are to learn and what they already know. To ignore students' experience in the classroom is a way of dismissing it and digging a chasm between the culture of the students and the culture of the school. More fundamentally, the development of democratic citizenship depends upon students seeing the connection between what they are learning and the world beyond the classroom. In this sense, learning is for use, not in the narrowly vocational sense, but in the sense that it helps to create an understanding of the way the world is and of how it might be. Célestin Freinet is eloquent on this question in his comparison of the school as temple, as barracks, and as a place of productive work (Freinet, 1990a, pp. 125-30). Even Matthew Arnold, the most eloquent defender of the view that worthwhile learning consisted of learning the best that has been known and written, did so not simply because such knowledge was good in itself, but because it helped to create a critical outlook. Mere knowledge, said Arnold, while important, was not enough: it must feed "... the noble aspiration to leave the world better and happier than we found it" (Arnold, 1859).

What we teach, and how we teach it, must help students to examine the world in which they live. This does not mean that the curriculum must consist of nothing but current events, nor does it mean that students should study nothing but what arises in their own lives, though some proponents of the concept of a distinctively working-class curriculum have at times come close to saying this. A.H. Halsey, for example, writing of English inner-city schools in Educational Priority Areas (EPA's) has argued:

> If we are concerned with the majority of children who will spend their lives in EPA's, rather than only with the minority who will leave them for universities and colleges and middle-class occupations elsewhere, then the schools must set out to equip their children to meet the grim reality of the social envi-

> ronment in which they live and reform it in all its aspects... only if they are armed with intimate familiarity with their immediate problems may they be expected to articulate the needs they feel and create the means for satisfying them. (Halsey, 1972:114)

One can see the point that Halsey is making, but there is a danger here that such a curriculum will deal only with the here and now, with what is immediately present and local, so that the world outside the classroom becomes the curriculum.

Dewey made a similarly ambiguous point when he argued that the curriculum must always begin with the student's experience: "One consideration stands out clearly when education is conceived in terms of experience. Anything which can be called a study, whether arithmetic, history, geography, or one of the natural sciences, must be derived from materials which at the outset fall within the scope of life experience." (Dewey, 1938:73) Dewey insisted upon "... the necessity of an actual, empirical situation as the initiating phase of thought," saying of history and geography in particular, "Even for older students, the social sciences would be less abstract and formal if they were dealt with less as sciences... and more in their direct subject-matter as that is found in the daily life of the social groups in which the student shares" (Dewey, 1916:153/201). As with Halsey, there is a suggestion here that the curriculum and life-experience should become one and the same.

However, as Kieran Egan has pointed out, life-experience is far more varied and much wider than the specifics of our daily lives. In Egan's words, "Before children can walk and talk, before they can skate or ride a bicycle, they know love and hate, pleasure and pain, joy and fear, good and bad, power and powerlessness, and the rhythms of expression and satisfaction, of hope and disappointment" (Egan, 1983:199). Egan's conclusion is that "... if our concern in education is with understanding the world and experience and the growth of knowledge about these, our beginning seems more sensibly based on children's grasp of the most fundamental categories of thought whereby these are made meaningful, rather than on their ability to walk and skate" (Egan, 1983:199). His point is well-taken. To call for a form of teaching that establishes links between the classroom and the world outside the school is not to call for a totally present-oriented curriculum dealing only with the here and now of students' experience. We are doing students no favours if we do not teach them history, literature, the arts, science and all the essentials of what is commonly called a liberal education. At the same time, this should not be done in a vacuum. What we teach, and how we teach it, must not ignore either what is happening in the world or the important themes of human experience.

Thus, to say that teachers must establish connections with the world outside the classroom does not mean abandoning such subjects as history or literature; nor does it mean that the curriculum must be based on some limited definition of relevance. There is almost nothing in the curriculum that cannot be used to illuminate the world in which we live. Good education demands that this be done. Democratic citizenship depends upon it. The native playwright, Tomson Highway, has noted of his education that it did not supplant his cultural tradition, but served to complement it: "... equipped... with the wisdom of Homer and Faulkner and Shakespeare and Bach and Beethoven and Rembrandt and McLuhan and many other thinkers, artists and philosophers of the white world, but equipped, as well, with the wisdom and vision of Big Bear and Black Elk and Chief Seattle and Tom Fiddler and Joe Highway and the medicine people, the visionaries of my ancestry — and the Cree language in all its power and beauty" (York, 1989:viii). This kind of empowerment is what we need for all students.

Some teachers are also developing more deliberate ways of combining work inside school with work outside it. This is done not only to strengthen the conventional curriculum but also to give students direct experience of working in and for the community. This is not one more item to be added to the existing curriculum, nor is it a diversion from the "basics" that are widely seen as so important. Rather, it is a vital part of a new approach to curriculum, providing an important educational experience both in its own right and in the contribution it can make to more traditional subjects.

In modern society, schools have too often cut children off from the world and, often with the best of intentions, denied them any possibility of making a useful contribution to society. The teenage years, in particular, have become a wasteland. They are a period of high energy and idealism, but we have effectively denied teenagers any useful role in society. As a U.S. report puts it: "... There is something wrong with our socialization process when adolescence, the stage of life during which energy and sometimes even idealization are highest, has become a time when waiting is the central task" (National Task Force, 1977:135). The words of the U.S. psychologist, Urie Bronfenbrenner, are worth considering in this regard, for what he says about the United States is equally applicable to Canada:

> Our children are not entrusted with any responsibilities; the ends and means have been determined by someone else and their job is to fulfil an assignment involving little judgment, decision-making, or risk. This practice is intended to protect children from burdens beyond their years, but there is reason to believe it has been carried too far. (Bronfenbrenner, 1974:60)

It is perhaps not surprising that in their survey of Canadian teenagers, Bibby and Posterski conclude that "Adults have set teenagers up for disenchantment and disappointment.... Stated simply, the problem is the failure of adults to let young people grow up. Expressed another way, adults suppress emergence" (Bibby & Posterski, 1985:4).

A large part of the solution to this problem is to close the gap that still often exists between the school and the world outside its walls, to establish some linkage between the curriculum and the community. In this regard, it is worth noting that the highly academic International Baccalaureate Program insists on students performing some form of community service, usually in the area of environmental protection (conservation, recycling and so on) or of working with young children, the poor, the handicapped or the elderly. In a similar vein, Educational Action Projects have been institutionalized in the French educational system to bring students into contact with their community through multi-discipliinary large group projects.

Such community work has obvious advantages. First, it helps students develop both a sense of community and the skills and disposition needed to make it effective. Second, it helps to empower students, to give them a sense of what Newmann calls "environmental competence." (Newmann, 1975). Third, it helps to eliminate the isolation and artificiality that so often characterize the curriculum. Fourth, it helps to provide the sense of motivation, purpose and commitment that teachers say is lacking in students. Fifth, it nurtures the kind of citizenship that we so desperately need today. And sixth, it can provide a valuable support to groups within the community who otherwise are isolated and helpless.

Community service can take many forms. They are limited only by the ingenuity of teachers and students. Examples include campaigning for community sports facilities; setting up recycling programmes; participating in a local political issue, e.g., regarding traffic regulations, pollution, urban development, vandalism; working in election campaigns; working with senior citizens; tutoring young children; compiling local histories; taking part in marches and demonstrations; working for UNICEF, Amnesty International or other such organizations; helping in a food bank. Such projects are organized not simply as activities in their own right, no matter how worthwhile, but as integral components of an educational plan. They are intended to help students learn both knowledge and skills, as well as having some impact on their values. They demand, for example, considerable planning and organization; research into problems; dealing with political realities; and a good deal of thought and discussion. Conrad and Hedin have proposed five criteria for assessing the worth of community service projects in schools. One, students have some responsibility for making their own decisions. Two, they should have other people depend on their activities, since this provides real responsibility. Three, they should work on tasks that demand thinking. Four, they should work with age groups other than their own. And five, they should be expected to reflect systematically on their experience (Conrad & Hedin, 1977).

Above all, such projects must be designed to produce the democratic citizenship that is the subject of this book. Good works, such as visiting the sick and the elderly, are certainly not to be despised, but they can easily be shorn of any social or political analysis and take on an aura of old-style charity visiting. This form of community service can be used to produce the kind of "responsible" citizenship so beloved of conservatives, consisting of doing one's bit to soften the rough edges of society without ever asking any of the tough questions about how they came to be there in the first place. It is not coincidental that the Thatcher government in the United Kingdom looked kindly upon what it called citizenship education, emphasizing good deeds and socially useful work but carefully separating them from any kind of political analysis. The aim of this approach to citizenship education is not empowerment but consensus and social peace. Its central message is that there is nothing in society that cannot be put right with a little good will and mutual effort.

The role of community service in democratic citizenship, however, is much different. It does not ignore the importance of good works and of helping others, but in doing so it also does not ignore the tough questions: How did things get to be this way? Do they have to be like this? What alternatives exist? How can we bring about change? Where is power located and how is it used? To ask these and similar questions immediately links community service with history and politics, with the social and natural sciences, and with other parts of the school curriculum.

One of the most appealing examples of linking the curriculum with the world outside the school, is Eliot Wigginton's *Foxfire* project in the United States. Wigginton found himself facing students for whom English and writing, and indeed just about everything else in the curriculum, had little to do with the world in which they lived in Georgia. He saw his first task as eliminating this sense of separation through a series of discussions and conversations on the question of what writing is for: "You make a list of all the places you see in the real world. And sometimes that list is hundreds of items long. When the students see the array of stuff that's possible, they make a connection between writing and the real world" (Wigginton, 1990:31). This led to the second question that he put to his students: "Okay, pick one, what do you want to do?" They chose magazines and thought long and hard about what should be in them, ending up with the idea of a magazine, *Foxfire*, that would concentrate on local material: interviews, crafts, superstitions, history, folklore and so on. After this, students moved on to other questions: How would they do it? How would they produce and distribute it? What would it cost? Where would they find the money? Who would do what? The first *Foxfire* book appeared in 1972, and *Foxfire* has been going strong ever since, resulting in books written and designed by students. In Wigginton's words: "... you can get students to the point where they can, in fact, write a book that is going to be published. They don't have to wait until they get out of college after years of practice, to do something like that. What they are involved in is not practice but doing things for real consumption by the outside world" (Wigginton, 1990:32). Wigginton's students are also involved in interviewing, researching, photographing, recording, writing, designing and performing countless other activities that involve them in both the community and the classroom.

Not every teacher can manage a *Foxfire*, but there are many less ambitious ways to bridge the chasm that too easily exists between the curriculum and the world. It would be an unimaginative teacher indeed who could do nothing with the events of today's world, even within the confines of a provincial curriculum. However it is done, the basic point is straightforward: we must connect what we do in the classroom with what is happening in the world at large.

9. Classrooms Must Be Characterized By Trust And Openness So That Students Find It Easy To Participate In Their Own Learning

Most classrooms are fairly passive places in which students have little voice or influence. Teachers are the controlling force and students largely learn to follow directions. Often they come to accept this as natural. According to one English study, "... children expect the teacher to act as the boss; to direct, initiate and control learning; to be judge and jury of work and conduct" (Hanson & Hetherington, 1976:568). For many students school has become a ritual, which they put up with either because they have no choice or because they want the diploma that it offers. In Bob Davis' words referred to earlier, "... schools are making working-class students dumb and middle-class students numb" (Davis, 1990:13). In the United States, Theodore Sizer has found that some teachers more or less accept the inevitability of this process. He has noted the existence of what he calls "Horace's compromise": a process by which teachers and students reach an unspoken agreement. The teacher agrees not to challenge or provoke the students and to accept a low standard of work. In return, the students accept the teacher, offer their cooperation (more or less), and generally avoid or dilute any academic challenge. It is not clear to what extent this is true of Canadian schools, but it is certain that we have not avoided it completely. One of the most disturbing findings of recent research on schools is not so much that students do not find schools all that interesting or exciting, but that they do not even expect them to be.

This is obviously unacceptable for a number of reasons. First, it destroys the possibility of schools offering their students a genuinely educational experience. An elementary school report card, for example, that reports to parents how their children are faring in matters of general behaviour (of school citizenship, in fact), does so using these headings: gets along with others; uses time to good advantage; completes assignments; works quietly and independently; listens well; is dependable; produces neat work; and, takes criticism and disappointment well. A junior-high school example is very similar, using these headings: assignments well done; well-prepared; good behavior; contributes in discussion; working below capability; doing all he/she can; inattentive; descriptive; seems interested. It should be remembered that these headings are from school report cards. They represent the public face of the school, describing those things that schools think are important enough to report to parents. They emphasize a set of qualities that are particularly passive. If, in fact, students do leave school with these characteristics, every Chamber of Commerce in the country should be delighted. They will be, from an employer's point of view, perfect workers: diligent, dutiful, able to take criticism and disappointment, free from "unrealistic" expectations and, no doubt, most unlikely to join unions or to rock the corporate boat. More is involved, however, than what is on the report cards. What they omit is equally striking. Given that they are educational documents, presumably reflecting a school's philosophy, it is incredible that they say nothing at all about such fundamental educational (and citizenship) values as creativity, originality, autonomy, and critical thinking.

The same pattern can been seen in school disciplinary systems and codes of rules, where the prevailing message is that students are not to be trusted and must, above all, be controlled. The most blatant example of this is assertive discipline, described in chapter 1, but it can be found in most of the approaches to rules and discipline used in schools. It is not without significance that books about discipline bear such titles as: *Changing Student Behavior*; *Help! These Kids Are Driving Me Crazy!*; *Survival Kit For Teachers*; *Making It Till Friday*. Obviously there is intended to be humour here, but such titles convey a view of schools as a battleground in which wary teachers fight for their survival against the hosts of rebellious students determined to do them down. Hence, no doubt, the widespread popularity of that old disciplinary adage: don't smile till Christmas. The central message of school discipline is typified in these words:

> The majority of these classroom rules, like the rules which govern our society, are designed for the common good. In order for large groups of people to live within a limited area, each individual must be socialized to certain rules of conduct or behavior. The teacher's source of control is directly dependent upon her (*sic*) ability to make rules and enforce the student's compliance with the rules. (Dollar, 1972:50)

Amazingly, these words are taken from a book called *Humanizing Classroom Discipline*. The key words leap from the paragraph: socialized, control, enforce, compliance. The assumptions are far from self-evident. Is it so certain that classroom rules are necessarily designed for the common good? And who decides what this is? Should we simply assume that only the teacher should make rules? Is there no room for students to have a voice? Should the teacher's source of control depend upon the ability to make rules and enforce compliance? Could it not — ought it not — arise from the teacher's knowledge and skill, and from her or his concern and care for students?

There are, admittedly, more genuinely educational approaches to discipline, and it cannot be denied that discipline is an important concern for teachers. Nothing can be usefully taught and learned unless students cooperate with each other and with their teacher. But to criticize existing disciplinary practice and to call for a more educational alternative, is not to advocate anarchy in the classroom. There is a lot of territory between the two extremes of the classroom as bootcamp and the classroom as blackboard jungle.

At the same time, if classrooms are to be characterized by trust and openness, the question of discipline cannot be ignored, if only because it is common for disciplinary rules and regulations to convey the message that students are not in fact to be trusted. Even when this is avoided, it is still possible for disciplinary needs and practices to create distrust between teachers and students. And students are not automatically or instinctively cooperative. Their immaturity and their impulsiveness will lead them necessarily to question, to challenge and in one way or another, to rebel. It is too easy to make the facile liberal assumption that students will automatically respond to their teacher's sincerity and goodwill.

There is, then, a certain amount of tension between the demands of control and the need to create a climate of trust and openness in the classroom. Control is necessary for learning to take place, but if learning is to be worthwhile it must result from the kind of personal commitment and conviction that is possible only in a climate of trust. Fortunately, although this tension exists, there are ways of resolving it, as shown by the example of successful classrooms around the country.

One can sense such classrooms almost immediately upon

entering them. More often than not, the room presents an attractive physical appearance. It is light and bright and colourful. There are pictures and posters on the walls, usually connected with the subjects being taught. Students' work is also on display. There may be plants and other such friendly touches. Books and magazines and other materials and equipment are plentiful, on shelves and ledges and anywhere there is space. Everything conveys the message that this is a place for learning and that learning is not a matter of cloistered seriousness, but a natural part of living.

Within this physical setting, in which the visual signals are so important, the students immediately strike the visitor as relaxed and friendly. They ask who you are and why you are there, but in a style that indicates interest and curiosity, not defensiveness or suspicion. They quickly accept your presence and either incorporate you into what they are doing (at the younger ages) or simply take your presence for granted. They are not at all disturbed or put out by the presence of a stranger. There is often a buzz of conversation, except when the task at hand calls for silence, but it is conversation that is largely related to the work being done, though still including an element of casual talk. Most strikingly, students know when they can talk and when they should keep quiet: when the teacher calls for order, they respond without having to be shouted at. They work well together, talking both seriously and socially, and often with a degree of humour and friendly insult that is the mark of acceptance and respect. They speak to their teacher without fear or antagonism. They are not afraid to ask questions, nor to state an objection or make a point, and they do so without belligerence or fawning. They know the routines of the classroom and use them easily, moving to the bookshelf to look up a reference, leaving their seat to get paper or perform some errand, leaving the room when they need to, all without fuss or disruption or having to seek special permission.

Many of these attitudes are found also in the teacher. He or she greets you when you show up at the classroom, and sees you as neither a threat nor an intrusion. Having welcomed you, and perhaps introduced you to the students, she or he goes about work as though you were not there. She or he is relaxed and confident enough not to be bothered by your presence: attention is focused upon the students and the task at hand. The teacher works easily with the students, making the odd joke here and there, engaging in some banter perhaps, but always keeping things moving. It is obvious from the teacher's comments that he or she knows the students as individuals, learning something about their lives, their interests, their families. The teacher handles interruptions without a fuss, and it soon dawns on you that she or he avoids most interruptions by anticipating them. A comment to a student here, a direction or suggestion there, serve to keep everyone focused on the task at hand. Above all, you notice the teacher frequently scanning the room; he or she has a knack of talking to the whole class as though talking to each student individually. The teacher's voice is clear and expressive. Explanations are clear and interesting. He or she uses comparison and analogy. Material that students had learned in earlier lessons is incorporated. It is immediately obvious that the teacher thinks that what she or he is teaching matters, that it is important to him or her personally, and therefore will probably also be seen by students in the same way.

Such classrooms exist. They can be found in almost any school. The question is, of course, how they come into being. Do they depend on the intuitive gifts of the born teacher or can they be made? Fortunately, the evidence suggests very strongly that the latter is the case and that most teachers can, with time and training, organize such classrooms.

Probably the easiest step to take concerns the furnishing and equipping of the classroom. It does not take much effort or imagination to give a classroom the physical appearance that proclaims it to be a user-friendly place. Posters, pictures, decorations, magazines, books, clippings-files, plants and furnishings — all help to establish the classroom as a special place and to deliver a message to students when they enter. Best of all is to involve students in equipping and maintaining the classroom. They can help to choose posters and pictures, they can paint murals, they can maintain clippings-files, and so on. All such activity helps to show students that the room is *their* room and that they have a stake in it. It also helps to show that they have a teacher who is willing to go beyond the bare essentials. When Hodgetts surveyed history teaching across Canada in the late 1960's, he found that the best teaching was being done in what he called social studies laboratories, rooms equipped with books, maps, equipment, models and the rest, all of which proclaimed them to be special places for the teaching of social studies (Hodgetts, 1968).

Physical decor and equipment will not of themselves establish a climate of trust and openness in the classroom, although they will go some way towards it. By far the greater part of the task will depend on the behaviour and attitudes of the students themselves. What is required is that students feel a sense of ownership of the classroom. Special training might need to be provided, for example in discussion and group-work, for students to work effectively together, but much will be accomplished by the force of the teacher's example and by the teacher's steady persistence in encouraging the kind of behaviour that is desired. Once students see what they are learning as important, interesting and worthwhile, and once they are given some voice in their own learning — the purposes of the pedagogy that is the subject of this book — many discipline problems will disappear.

There will, however, still be occasion for discipline in the form of control. Not all students will be cooperative all the time. There will inevitably be disruptive incidents and teachers must be able to deal with them.

In even the best-run school and the most stimulating classroom, discipline problems are likely to occur from time to time and, unless one adopts the hands-off policies that characterized Summerhill, something will have to be done about them. Aside from taking whatever action is necessary in the short term simply to stop disruption, the first and most important step to take is to start making distinctions. One kind of overt action, such as rudeness or disruptiveness for instance, can spring from many different causes. And different causes imply different treatments. Discipline problems may be caused by any of the following:

1. Viciousness; e.g. a calculated, deliberate provocation.
2. Power-play; e.g. an attempt by a student or students to control the class, such as sometimes happens to substitute teachers.
3. Ebullience; e.g. an inability to stop "horsing around", a constant playing of the clown.
4. Ignorance; e.g., when a student simply does not know any better or different way of behaving.
5. Boredom; e.g. an inability to find anything in the lesson, or indeed in the school, of interest or significance.
6. Thoughtlessness; e.g. when a student does something without thinking.
7. Distraction; e.g. when students' minds are still on a previous lesson or activity.
8. Emotional upset; e.g. the death of a relative or friend.

The point about such a list — and many others could be drawn up — is that it helps the teacher focus on the cause of the behaviour in question and that it implies a series of different remedies. Generally, the list appears in order of decreasing seriousness. It would be a harsh teacher, for example, who would do much about misbehaviour arising from ignorance or thoughtlessness, except to speak to the student and explain what was expected. Misbehaviour arising from boredom, on the other hand, suggests a careful rethinking of curriculum content and teaching strategies. If a particular novel, for instance, has no appeal for students and if all attempts to make it interesting are unsuccessful, then perhaps there is an alternative. If a particular social studies topic provokes yawns and indifference, perhaps the time allotted to it can be reduced in order to give more time to something more interesting. After all, if students are not learning anything, it hardly seems worthwhile to persist. And, if they are not learning anything of interest through the subject-matter, students may well look for ways of adding spice to the lesson, thus creating discipline problems. This is not to say that students be taught only what interests them or that the curriculum should be decided by a daily vote. Usually, teaching strategies that inspire student involvement and input will produce interest even if the topics themselves are not particularly exciting.

It must be admitted that there are classes where discipline problems, even the minor ones, are so abundant that no effective learning or teaching can take place. We all know the classroom in which students move from seat to seat, talk to each other at will, throw erasers, balls of paper and other objects, retire into their own private worlds, and generally make it plain that their minds are anywhere but on the lesson. There are various responses to this kind of situation. One is simply to give up, in view of the magnitude of the problems, and to write off the students as unmotivated or non-academic. Another is to try and teach as though nothing untoward is happening and to concentrate on the students who appear to be paying attention. Another is to find some way of keeping students occupied, usually with plenty of busy-work consisting of completing worksheets or copying notes from the overhead projector, and punctuated by reminders that the topic is important because "it will be on the test." One can sympathize with all these approaches: they are understandable ways by which teachers can cope with unbearable situations. Nonetheless, the fact remains that all of them are destructive because they avoid the necessity of asking radical questions about curriculum and teaching strategies.

Sometimes, of course, the problem will lie not with the curriculum or the teaching, but in social and economic conditions over which teachers have little or no control. For instance, it is not easy for students suffering from racial discrimination, from parental neglect, or from all the accumulated effects of poverty, to take a lively interest in their school work. There is not a great deal that schools acting on their own can do about these kinds of problems, but they can at least begin to tackle them by working in conjunction with community agencies and parents.

Obviously it is better to prevent discipline problems from ever arising than to have to deal with them after the fact.

Although it is unlikely that we shall ever reach this state of perfection, it remains true that many discipline problems occur needlessly and could have been prevented with a little forethought.

Some researchers have identified personal qualities of teachers that can minimize discipline problems. Of these, the most useful is J.S. Kounin's research, which concentrates on three qualities: "with-itness"; "overlappingness"; and ease of transition. By "with-itness," Kounin means the quality of knowing what is going on in a classroom (having eyes in the back of one's head) and, equally important, demonstrating to all involved that one knows what is going on. "Overlappingness" describes the quality of being able to attend to two (or more) things at once, perhaps working with one group of students while scanning others, or monitoring the class while attending to a visitor at the door. "Ease of transition" refers to the ability to move from one phase of a lesson to another clearly and smoothly and avoiding distraction (Kounin, 1970).

All such prescriptions, however, while useful, are more or less mechanical formulations of what should be basic interaction between teachers and students. Nothing can substitute for an interesting lesson, well-taught, on a worthwhile topic. Good teaching and a relevant curriculum remain the answer to most discipline problems.

Above all, we must organize our classrooms so that we teach as much by example as by direct message. We must recognize that classroom climate or atmosphere is a vital part of any pedagogy. In Toronto, for example, the Parents for Peace emphasized the importance of the "peaceful classroom," which would encourage students to "... decrease competition and increase cooperation, to still aggression and promote helpfulness, to divert ostracism and encourage acceptance." The peaceful classroom is organized upon these principles:

1. Students must see the classroom as belonging to them, not only to the teacher.

2. Teachers and students must use problem-solving approaches in which they work together.

3. There must be mutual respect amongst everyone in the classroom, students and teacher alike.

The Parents for Peace went on to suggest how this could be implemented, suggesting six criteria by which to judge whether or not classroom activities are appropriate. First, work must allow for student choice. Second, self-expression must be encouraged. Third, cooperative activities must be emphasized. Fourth, activities must promote a sense of self-worth. Fifth, students must be involved in the exploration of social values. Sixth, learning must be connected with the real world outside the classroom.

Part of the solution is to redefine the role of students. They have to cease being the more or less passive recipients of someone else's information and begin to see their own ideas as worth examining. For if we have often persuaded ourselves that youngsters know very little that is worth knowing, we have at the same time persuaded the youngsters themselves that this is indeed true. Unless they refuse to play the school game, they quickly come to see themselves as consumers of information. Hence, that all too familiar question: "Will this be in the test?" Instead, we need to take seriously this definition of relevance:

> Relevance is not a matter of adapting a subject to the apparent interests of a pupil or to the apparent fashions of the moment. Relevance is achieved by assuming that a pupil or students has something to contribute to the subject. Relevance at its deepest has nothing to do with subject matter; it has to do with the status of the learner in relation to what is being learned. (Mason, 1977:107)

And if we can change the status of the learners, we will do more than affect their position as students. We will have an impact on the way they see their world and their position within it. We will be teaching for democratic citizenship.

Bibliography

Almond, G. & S. Verba. *The Civic Culture.* Boston: Little, Brown, 1965.

Arnold, M. *Culture and Anarchy.* Cambridge University Press, 1950 (first published 1869).

Aronson, E. *The Jigsaw Classroom.* Beverley Hills: Sage, 1978.

Ashton-Warner, S. *Teacher.* New York: Simon & Schuster, 1963.

Barnes, Douglas. *From Communication to Curriculum,* Harmondsworth: Penguin Books, 1976.

Belenkey, M. et al. *Women's Ways of Knowing.* New York: Basic Books, 1986.

Bennett, N. *Teaching Styles and Pupil Progress.* Cambridge: Harvard University Press, 1976.

Benton, M. & Fox, G. *Teaching Literature: Nine to Fourteen.* Oxford: Oxford University Press, 1985.

Beyer, B.K. *Developing a Thinking Skills Program.* Boston: Allyn & Bacon, 1988.

Beyer, B.K. *Practical Strategies for the Teaching of Thinking.* Boston: Allyn & Bacon, 1988.

Bibby, R.W. & Posterski D.C. *The Emerging Generation: An Inside Look at Canada's Teenagers.* Toronto: Irwin, 1985.

Blair, J.A. "The Keegstra Affair." *The History and Social Science Teacher,* 21(3), March 1986, 158-164.

Bossert, S. *Tasks and Social Relationships in Classrooms.* Cambridge: Cambridge University Press, 1979

Botkin, F.W., et al. *No Limits to Learning*. Oxford: Pergamon, 1979.

Bowles, S. & Gintis H. *Schooling in Capitalist America.* New York: Basic Books, 1976.

Boyd, W. *The Educational Thought of Jean-Jacques Rousseau.* New York: 1963.

Brophy, J. & Good T. "Teacher Behaviour and Student Achievement," in M.C. Wittrock (*ed.*), *Handbook of Research on Teaching*. New York: Macmillan, 1986.

Bronfenbrenner, U. "The Origins of Alienation." *Scientific American* 231 (1974) 53-6.

Bruner, J.S. *The Relevance of Education.* New York: Norton, 1971.

Bruner, J.S. *In Search of Mind.* New York: Harper & Row 1983.

Bullock, A. *The Humanist Tradition in the West.* New York: Norton, 1985.

Clandfield, David, "Pacijou and the War-Toys Project in Québec", *Our Schools/Our Selves*, II, 2 (April 1990) and II, 3 (September 1990).

Cohen, P. "Against the New Vocationalism," in I. Bates et al. (eds.), *Schooling for the Dole*? London: Macmillan, 1984.

Cole, M. (ed.). *Bowles and Gintis Revisited.* Lewes: Falmer Press, 1988.

Connell, R. *Making the Difference: Schools, Families and Social Division.* Sydney: Allen & Unwin, 1982.

Conrad, D.C. & Hedin D. "Learning and Earning Citizenship Through Participation," in J. Shaver (ed.), *Building Rationales for Citizenship Education.* Washington: National Council for the Social Studies, 1977, 48-73.

Cook, R. *Canada, Quebec and the Uses of Nationalism*. Toronto: McClelland & Stewart, 1987.

Culley, M. & Portuges C. *Gendered Subjects: The Dynamics of Feminist Teaching*. London: Routledge & Kegan Paul, 1985.

Culley, M. "Feminist Pedagogy: Lost Voices of American Women," in L. Hoffman & D. Rosenfelt, (eds.), *Teaching Women's Literature From A Regional Perspective.* New York: Modern Language Association, 1982.

Dale, R. (ed.). *Schooling and Capitalism.* London: Routledge & Kegan Paul, 1976.

Davis, B. *What Our High Schools Could Be.* Toronto: Our Schools, Our Selves, 1990.

de Bono, E. *de Bono's Thinking Course.* New York: Facts on File, 1982.

Dewey, J. *The Child and the Curriculum (1902) and the School and Society (1899).* Chicago: University of Chicago Press, 1956.

Dewey, J. *Democracy and Education,* New York: Macmillan, 1916.

Dewey, J. *Experience and Education (1938).* New York: Collier, 1963.

Dollar, B. *Humanizing Classroom Discipline.* New York: Harper & Row, 1972.

Dreeben, R. *On What Is Learned In School.* Reading: Addison-Wesley, 1968.

Eby, F. *The Development of Modern Education.* Englewood Cliffs: Prentice Hall, 1952.

Egan, K. *Educational Development.* New York: Oxford University Press, 1979.

Egan, K. *Education and Psychology: Plato, Piaget and Scientific Psychology.* New York: Teachers College Press, 1983.

Ennis, R. "A Concept of Critical Thinking." *Harvard Educational Review,* 32(1), (1962) 81-111.

Fawcett Hill, W. *Learning Thru Discussion.* Beverley Hills: Sage, 1962.

Fenton, E. *The New Social Studies.* New York: Holt, Rinehart & Winston, 1968.

Freinet, Célestin. 1990a, *The Wisdom of Mathew.* Lewiston/Queenston: Edwin Mellon Press, 1990.

Freinet, Célestin. 1990b, *Cooperative Learning & Social Change. Selected Writings of Célestin Freinet.* Toronto: Our Schools/Our Selves, 1990.

Freire, P. *Pedagogy of the Oppressed.* New York: Continuum, 1970.

French, M. *Beyond Power: On Women, Men and Morals.* New

York, Summit, 1985.

Gaskell, J., A. McLaren, & M. Novogrodsky. *Claiming An Education: Feminism and Canadian Schools.* Toronto: Our Schools, Our Selves, 1989.

Gellner, G. *Plough, Sword and Book: The Structure of Human History.* London: Collins, 1988.

Gilligan, C. *In A Different Voice.* Cambridge: Harvard University Press, 1982.

Gilligan, C. et al. *Mapping the Moral Domain: A Contribution of Women's Thinking to Psychological Theory and Education.* Cambridge: Harvard University Press, 1988.

Gilligan, C. *et al. Making Connections: the Relational Worlds of Adolescent Girls at Emma Willard School.* Cambridge: Harvard University Press, 1990.

Giroux, H. *Schooling and the Struggle for Public Life: Critical Pedagogy in the Modern Age.* Minneapolis: University of Minnesota Press, 1988.

Giroux, H. *Ideology, Culture and the Process of Schooling.* Philadelphia: Temple University Press, 1981.

Giroux, H. "Public Philosophy and the Crisis in Education." *Harvard Educational Review,* 42 (1984), 186-194.

Giroux, H. "Marxism and Schooling: The Limits of Radical Discourse." *Educational Theory,* 34 (1984), 113-135.

Giroux, H. "The Hope of Radical Education." *Journal of Education,* 170 (1988), 91-101

Giroux, H. & McLaren P. *Critical Pedagogy, the State, and Cultural Struggle.* Albany: State University of New York Press, 1989.

Giroux, H. & Simon R. (eds.). *Popular Culture, Schooling and Everyday Life.* Toronto: O.I.S.E. Press, 1989.

Halsey, A.H. *Educational Priority Areas.* London: H.M.S.O., 1972.

Hanson, D. & M. Herrington. "Please, Miss, You're Supposed to Stop Her." *New Society,* 10 June, 1976.

Hargreaves, D. *The Challenge of the Comprehensive School.* London: Routledge & Kegan Paul, 1982.

Harris, K. *Teachers and Classes: A Marxist Analysis*. London: Routledge & Kegan Paul, 1982.

Heater, D.B. *Citizenship*. London: Longmans, 1990.

Henley, R. & Pampallis J. "The Campaign for Compulsory Education in Manitoba." *Canadian Journal of Education*, 7 (1), 1987, 59-83.

Hirsch, E.D. *Cultural Literacy: What Every American Needs to Know*. New York: Random House, 1988.

Hobsbawm, E. & Ranger T. (eds.). *The Invention of Tradition*. Cambridge: Cambridge University Press, 1982.

Hodgetts, A.B. *What Culture? What Heritage?* Toronto: O.I.S.E., 1968.

Hoffnung, M. *Feminist Transformations: Teaching Experimental Psychology*. Wellesley College Center for Women's Studies, Working Paper #140, 1984.

Jackson, P. *Life in Classrooms*. New York: Holt, Rinehart & Winston, 1968.

Johnson, D.W. & Johnson R. "Social Skills for Successful Group Work." *Educational Leadership*, Dec. 1989-Jan. 1990.

Johnson, D.W. & Johnson R. *Learning Together and Alone*. Englewood Cliffs: Prentice-Hall, 1975.

Keddie, N. "Classroom Knowledge," in M.F.D. Young (ed.), *Knowledge and Control*. London: Collier Macmillan, 1971, 133-160.

Kelly, J. *Women, History and Theory*. Chicago: University of Chicago Press, 1984.

Knowles, D. *The Evolution of Medieval Thought*. New York: Knopf, 1962.

Kohl, H. *Growing Minds: On Becoming A Teacher*. New York: Harper & Row, 1984.

Kohl, H. *I Won't Learn From You: The Role of Assent in Learning*. Minneapolis: Milkweed Editions, 1991.

Kounin, J. *Discipline and Group Management in Schools*. New York: Holt, Rinehart & Winston, 1970.

Lightfoot, S. "Politics and Reasoning Through the Eyes of Teachers and Children." *Harvard Educational Review*, 43, 1973, 197-244.

Lipman, M., Sharp A.M., Oscanyan F.S. *Philosophy in the Classroom.* Montclair: Institute for the Advancement of Philosophy for Children, 1977.

Maîtresse d'école, La. *Building a People's Curriculum.* Toronto: Our Schools/Our Selves, 1989.

Martin, J.R. *Reclaiming A Conversation: The Ideal of the Educated Woman.* New Haven: Yale University Press, 1985.

Martin, J.R. "Reforming Teacher Education, Rethinking Liberal Education." *Teachers' College Record*, 88 (1987), 406-409.

Mason, E. "A-Level History." *History Workshop Journal*, 3, 1977, 105-109.

Massialas, B. & Cox C. *Inquiry in the Social Studies Classroom.* New York: McGraw-Hill, 1966.

McIntosh, P. *Interactive Phases of Curricular Re-Vision: A Feminist Perspective.* Wellesley College Centre for Research on Women: Working Paper #24, 1983.

McLaren, P. *Life in Schools.* Toronto: Irwin , 1989.

Mishler, W. *Political Participation in Canada.* Toronto: McGraw-Hill-Ryerson, 1979.

National Task Force on Citizenship Education. *Education for Responsible Citizenship.* New York: McGraw-Hill, 1977.

Newmann, F. *Education for Citizen Action.* Berkeley: McCutchan, 1975.

Nyquist, E.B. & Hawes G.R. (*eds.*). *Open Education: A Sourcebook for Parents and Teachers.* New York: Bantam, 1972.

Oakes, J. & Lipton M. *Making the Best of Schools.* New Haven: Yale University Press, 1990.

Okin, S.M. *Women in Western Political Thought.* Princeton: Princeton University Press, 1979.

Orwell, G. "Such, Such, Were the Joys," in *The Collected Essays, Journalism, and Letters of George Orwell.* London: Secker & Warburg, 1968.

Osborne, K. "Some Psychological Concerns For the Teaching of History." *The History and Social Science Teacher*, X, 1975, 15-25.

Osborne, K. *"Hard-working, Temperate and Peaceable" : The Portrayal of Workers in Canadian History Textbooks*. Winnipeg: University of Manitoba Education Monographs, 1981.

Osborne, K. *Educating Citizens: A Democratic Socialist Agenda for Canadian Education.* Toronto: Our Schools, Our Selves, 1988.

Parents for Peace. *Teaching for Peace: A Rationale and Activities for the Elementary School.* Toronto: Toronto Board of Education, 1985.

Parsons, T. "The School Class as a Social System," *Harvard Educational Review*, 29 (1959), 297-318.

Paul, R. et al. *Critical Thinking Handbook.* Sonoma State University: Center for Critical Thinking and Moral Critique, 1989.

Prentice, A. et al. *Canadian Women: A History.* Toronto: Harcourt, Brace, Jovanovich, 1988.

Radwanski, G. *The Relevance of Education and the Issue of Drop-outs.* Toronto: Ontario Ministry of Education, 1987.

Raths, J.D. "Teaching Without Specific Objectives," *Educational Leadership*, April, 1971, 714-720.

Rist, R.C. *The Urban School: Factory for Failure.* Cambridge: M.I.T. Press, 1973.

Rogers, C. *Freedom to Learn.* Columbus: Merrill, 1969.

Rosenshine, B. & Stevens R. "Teaching Functions," in M.C. Wittrock (ed.), *Handbook of Research on Teaching.* New York: Macmillan, 1986.

Rosenthal, R. & Jacobson L. *Pygmalion in the Classroom.* New York: Holt, Rinehart & Winston, 1968.

Rousseau, J.J. *The Social Contract* (1762), London: Dent Everyman's Library, 1911.

Rusk, R.R. *Doctrines of the Great Educators.* New York: Macmillan, 1957.

Sawyer, D. *Tomorrow Is School.* Toronto: McClelland & Stewart, 1979.

Scheir, W. & Scheir M. "The Joy of Learning — in the Open Corridor." *New York Times Magazine*, 4 April, 1971.

Schniedewind, N. "Feminist Values: Guidelines for Teaching Methodology in Women's Studies," in C. Bunch & S. Pollack (eds.), *Learning our Way: Essays in Feminist Education.* Trumansburg: Crossing Press, 1983, 261-271.

Shor, I. & Freire P. *A Pedagogy for Liberation.* South Hadley: Bergin & Garvey, 1987.

Shrewsbury C.M. "What is Feminist Pedagogy?" *Women's Studies Quarterly*, 15 (1987).

Siegel, H. *Educating Reason.* New York: Routledge, 1988.

Silberman, C. *Crisis in the Classroom.* New York: Vintage, 1970.

Slavin, R.E., et al. *Learning to Cooperate: Cooperating To Learn.* New York: Plenum, 1985.

Slavin, R.E., et al. "Cooperative Learning Models for the 3 R's." *Educational Leadership*, Dec., 1989/Jan. 1990.

Simon, R. "Critical Pedagogy," in *International Encyclopedia of Education.* Oxford: Pergamon, 1985, 1119-1120.

Smith, D.E. *The Everyday World as Problematic: A Feminist Sociology.* Toronto: University of Toronto Press, 1987.

Smith, D.E. *The Conceptual Practices of Power: A Feminist Sociology of Power.* Toronto: University of Toronto Press, 1990.

Spender, D. (ed.). *Men's Studies Modified.* Oxford: Pergamon, 1981.

Torney, J.V. et al. *Civic Education in Ten Countries.* New York: Wiley, 1975.

Thompson, E.P. "Time, Work-discipline and Industrial Capitalism." *Past and Present*, 38 (1967), 56-97.

Webster, J. *Academiarum Examen* (1653) in A.G. Debus, *Science and Education in the 17th Century: the Webster-Ward Debate.* London: MacDonald, 1970.

Wells, H.G. *The New Machiavelli.* New York: Duffield, 1910.

Wells, H.G. *The Story of A Great Schoolmaster.* New York: Macmillan, 1924.

Williams, R. *Culture and Society.* Harmondsworth: Penguin, 1961.

Wigginton, E. "On 25 Years of Foxfire: A Conversation with Eliot Wigginton." *Educational Leadership*, March 1990, 31-35.

Willis, P. *Learning to Labour: How Working Class Kids Get Working Class Jobs.* Farnborough: Saxon House, 1976.

York, G. *The Dispossessed.* Toronto: Lester & Orpen Denys, 1989.

Young, M.F.D. (ed.). *Knowledge and Control.* London: Collier-Macmillan, 1971.

Yudkin, M. (ed.). *General Education.* Harmondsworth: Penguin, 1971.

Join The Debate On What Should Happen In Canada's Schools. You Can Still Get Your Own Copy Of Each Of These Issues Of Our Schools/Our Selves.

Issue #1: (Journal) A Feminist Agenda For Canadian Education ... The Saskatoon Native Survival School ... School Wars: BC, Alberta, Manitoba ... Contracting Out At The Toronto Board ... On Strike: Toronto Teachers And Saskatoon Profs ... Labour's Message in Nova Scotia Schools and Queen's Park ... The Free Trade Ratchet ...

Issue #2: Educating Citizens: A Democratic Socialist Agenda For Canadian Education by Ken Osborne. A coherent curriculum policy focussed on "active citizenship." Osborne takes on the issues of a "working-class curriculum" and a national "core" curriculum: what should student's know about Canada and the world at large?

Issue #3: (Journal) BC Teachers, Solidarity and Vander Zalm ... The Anti-Streaming Battle in Ontario ... The Dangers of School-Based Budgeting ... "Whole Language" in Nova Scotia ... Vancouver's Elementary Schools 1920-60 ... The Martimes in Song and Text ... Teaching "G-Level" Kids ... The Squeeze on Alberta's Teachers ... In Winnipeg: "The Green Slime Strikes Back!" ...

Issue #4: (Journal) Teaching The Real Stuff Of The World: Bears, History, Work Skills ... Tory Times At Sask Ed ... The NDP At The Toronto School Board ... Indian Control In Alberta Schools ... Is The Action Affirmative For Women School Board Workers ... Radwanski: The Dark Side ... More On "Whole Language" In Nova Scotia ... A Steelworker's Education ... B.C. Teachers Hang Tough ... Decoding Discrimination ...

Issue #5: Making A People's Curriculum: The Experience Of La maîtresse d'école edited with an introduction by David Clandfield. Since 1975 this Montreal teacher collective has been producing alternative francophone curricula on labour, human rights, peace, and geo-political issues in a framework of cooperative learning. This is an anthology of their best work.

Issue #6: (Journal) Labour Education And The Auto Workers ... Nova Scotia's Children Of The State ... Patrick Watson's *Democracy* ... Popular Roots Of The "New Literacy" ... Canada's Learner Centres ... Right Wing Thinking In Education ... Fighting Sexism In Nfld ... The Computer Bandwagon ... *Glasnost* and *Perestroika* Over Here? Funding Native Education ...

Issue #7: Claiming An Education: Feminism and Canadian Schools by Jane Gaskell, Arlene McLaren, Myra Novogrodsky. This book examines "equal opportunity," what students learn about women, what women learn about themselves and what has been accomplished by women who teach, as mothers and teachers.

Issue #8: It's Our Own Knowledge: Labour, Public Education & Skills Training by Julie Davis et al. The clearest expression yet of Labour's new educational agenda for the 1990s. It begins with working class experience in the schools and community colleges, takes issue with corporate initiatives in skills training, and proposes a program "for workers, not for bosses."

Issue #9: (Journal) Rekindling Literacy In Mozambique ... Privatizing The Community Colleges ... CUPE's Educational Agenda ... High Schools & Teenage Sex ... Workers And The Rise of Mass Schooling ... More On Nova Scotia's Children of the State ... Grade 1 Learning ... Private School Funding ... The Globe's Attack on Media Studies ... "Consolidation" in PEI ... Manitoba's High School Review ...

Issue #10: Heritage Languages: The Development And Denial Of Canada's Linguistic Resources by Jim Cummins and Marcel Danesi. This book opens up the issue of teaching heritage languages in our schools to a broad audience. It provides the historical context, analyzes opposing positions, examines the rationale and research support for heritage language promotion, and looks at the future of multiculturalism and multilingualism in Canada.

Issue #11: (Journal) No More War Toys: The Quebec Campaign ... Labelling the Under-Fives ... Building a Socialist Curriculum ... High School Streaming in Ontario ... Growing Up Male in Nova Scotia ... New Left Academics ... Tory Cutbacks in Alberta ... More On Workers And The Rise Of Mass Schooling ... The Elementary School Ruby And How High School Turned Her Sour ...

Double Issue #12-13: What Our High Schools Could Be: A Teacher's Reflections From The 60s To The 90s by Bob Davis. The author leads us where his experience has led him — as a teacher in a treatment centre for disturbed children, in an alternative community school, in a graduate education faculty, and for 23 years in two Metro Toronto high schools. The book ranges from powerful description to sharp analysis — from sex education to student streaming to the new skills mania.

Issue #14: (Journal) Feminism, Schools and the Union ... What's Happening in China's Schools ... NB Teacher Aides and the Struggle for Standards ... Barbie Dolls and Unicef ... Post-secondary Cuts in Alberta ... CUPE-Teacher Links ... Language Control In Nova Scotia ... Pay Equity For Ontario Teachers ... Women's Struggles/Men's Responsibility ...

Issue #15: Cooperative Learning And Social Change: Selected Writings Of Célestin Freinet edited and translated by David Clandfield and John Sivell. Célestin Freinet (1896-1966) pioneered an international movement for radical educational reform through cooperative learning. His pedagogy is as fresh and relevant today as it was in his own time, whether dealing with the importance of creative and useful work for children or linking schooling and community with wider issues of social justice and political action. This translation is the first to bring a broad selection of Freinet's work to an English-speaking audience.

Issue #16: (Journal) BC's Privatization Of Apprenticeship ... Marketing Adult Ed In Saskatchewan ... The Future Of Ontario's CAATs ... Edmonton's Catalyst Theatre ... The Money Crisis In Nova Scotia Schools ... The Politics Of Children's Literature ... Tough Kids Out Of Control ... A Literacy Policy For Newfoundland? ... Métis Schooldays ... Capitalism And Donald Duck ... In Struggle: Ontario Elementary Teachers ...

Issue #17: (Journal) Towards An Anti-Racist Curriculum ... Discovering Columbus ... The Baffin Writers' Project ... The Anti-Apartheid Struggle In South Africa's Schools ... What People Think About Schooling ... Children's Work ... Radical Literacy ... Getting the Gulf Into The Classroom ... Bye-Bye Minimum C Grades ... Taking Action On Aids ...

Issue #18: (Journal) Can The NDP Make A Difference?... Columbus In Children's Literature ... Labour Takes On Ontario's Education Bureaucrats ... Lessons From Yukon Schools ... Vision 2000 Revisited ... Getting A Feminist Education The Hard Way ... Children In Poverty ... Reflections Of A Lesbian Teacher ... Literacy, Politics and Religion in Newfoundland ... Critiquing The National Indicators ... Student Loans In Saskatchewan ...